PRACTICAL LANGUAGE

Editors: Marion Geddes and Gill

No. 3
Teaching Written English

PRACTICAL LANGUAGE TEACHING
Editors: Marion Geddes and Gill Sturtridge

1. *Planning and Using the Blackboard*
   Patricia Mugglestone
2. *Using the Magnetboard*
   Donn Byrne
3. *Teaching Written English*
   Ronald V. White
4. *The Magazine Picture Library*
   Janet McAlpin
5. *Using Blackboard Drawing*
   Peter Shaw and Thérèse de Vet
6. *Photograph Slides in Language Teaching*
   Angela Ayton and Margaret Morgan
7. *Video in the Language Classroom*
   Marion Geddes and Gill Sturtridge
8. *Using the Overhead Projector*
   J. R. H. Jones
9. *Teaching Reading Skills in a Foreign Language*
   Christine Nuttall
10. *Teaching Vocabulary*
    Michael J. Wallace

Teaching Written English

RONALD V. WHITE

HEINEMANN EDUCATIONAL BOOKS
London

Heinemann Educational Books Ltd
22 Bedford Square, London WC1B 3HH

LONDON EDINBURGH MELBOURNE AUCKLAND
HONG KONG SINGAPORE KUALA LUMPUR
NEW DELHI IBADAN NAIROBI JOHANNESBURG
PORTSMOUTH (NH) KINGSTON PORT OF SPAIN

© Ronald V. White
First published 1980
Reprinted with corrections 1983
Reprinted 1985, 1986

British Library Cataloguing in Publication Data

White, Ronald V
  Teaching written English.—Practical
language teaching; no. 3).
  1. English language—Text-books for
foreigners
  I. Title II. Series
  428'.2'4   PE1128   79-40960

ISBN 0 435 28968 3

Typeset in 10 on 12 point Times by Trade Linotype Ltd, Birmingham
and printed and bound in Great Britain by
Biddles Ltd, Guildford and King's Lynn

Contents

Acknowledgements	*page*	6
Terminology and Abbreviations		6

PART ONE

1	Introduction	7
2	The Status of Writing in ELT	8
3	What is Writing Like?	9
4	Types of Writing: Institutional and Personal	14
5	Conclusion: Implications for Teaching Writing	16

PART TWO

6	Types of Writing Exercises: False Cues	17
7	Good Cues: Bad Results	19
8	Reporting Past Events: Narrative	25
9	Describing Objects	42
10	Describing People	53
11	Describing Places	64
12	Describing Processes	75
13	Comparing and Recommending	83
14	Questions and Answers	92
15	Dictation and Writing	98
16	Integrating Reading, Speaking, Listening and Writing	104
17	Correcting Written Work	106
18	Summary	109
	References	110

Acknowledgements

I would like to thank the following for permission to use material:

The English Language Teaching Journal
Longman Cheshire Pty Ltd for extracts from *Village and Town in New Guinea*. R. B. Dakeyne (Case Studies in Australasian Geography 1)
Times Newspapers Ltd for the extract on p 53 which was reproduced from *The Sunday Times* Magazine, 15th May 1977
Nelson for reproduction of exercises and illustrations which appear in my book *Functional English* (Nelson 1979)
Swan National car rental
Rollei (UK) Ltd

Particular thanks are due to colleagues at the University of Manchester and the Centre for Applied Language Studies, University of Reading. Also to Michael Beaumont, a former student whose exercise on the noun group I have used in Section II on 'Describing Places', and finally to my wife Nora, I wish to express my gratitude for her unfailing support.

Terminology and Abbreviations

Base	=	Infinitive, e.g. live, arrive, travel
Base + s	=	3rd person Simple Present tense verb form, e.g. lives, arrives, travels
Base + ed	=	Preterite or Past Simple tense verb form, e.g. lived, arrived, travelled
Base + ing	=	Present Participle, e.g. living, arriving, travelling
Cl	=	Class of students
S	=	Individual student
SS	=	Students
BB	=	Blackboard (or chalkboard or whiteboard, depending on what you yourself use)
OHP	=	Overhead projector
ELT	=	English Language Teaching to non-native speakers of that language, subsuming EFL (English as a Foreign Language) and ESL (English as a Second Language)
ESP	=	English for Specific Purposes

Part One

1 INTRODUCTION

In this book I attempt to outline some ways of teaching writing, based on my own work and that of colleagues in ELT. I will not deal with the teaching of script, as this is a highly specialised area in which I can claim no expertise. If you are particularly concerned with this in your teaching, you will find some references at the end of the book.

Nor will I devote very much space to the teaching of such types of writing as personal letters, commercial correspondence, and so on. As I hope to show, there are some very good reasons for *not* attempting to do this in the general writing class. In any case, specialised fields such as commercial correspondence fall within the domain of English for Specific Purposes, and this is not a book on ESP.

Having learnt what this book will not cover, you will now want to know what I do deal with. Very simply, I attempt to suggest ways in which writing can be taught as a means of communication, in which formal correctness is linked to stylistic appropriateness, and in which the ability to write logically and grammatically connected sequences of sentences is fundamental. I hope that you will find my suggestions a useful starting point for selecting and adapting writing exercises from published sources as well as for developing ideas of your own.

2 THE STATUS OF WRITING IN ELT

For some time, under the influence of the audio-lingual approach to language teaching, it has been conventional wisdom to regard speech as being of primary importance, with writing being placed a poor second. Indeed, writing was regarded as being a somewhat inferior form of the language, a pale imitation of speech. When zealously applied, this viewpoint has had a number of unfortunate consequences for the learner. To begin with, he was often denied the support of the written language during the early phases of learning. This could be very frustrating to a literate adult, used to learning from written sources. Secondly, the learner who wished to acquire a reading and writing control of the language had to proceed through a lot of spoken practice before getting down to the written form. Thirdly, writing practice, when it was introduced, tended to be an extension of spoken practice even though, as is quite obvious when we think of it, we do not often write exactly what we say.

It would be foolhardy to claim that we have now reached an age of enlightenment and that we now know exactly how to teach writing. It would be true to say, however, that writing is no longer relegated to second place. Instead, writing is given its own status in the ELT course. There are a number of reasons for this. For one thing, linguists have become interested in studying the characteristics of written as well as spoken language, and it is now clear to everyone that writing is not simply a poor relative of speaking—or that speaking is merely a sloppy version of writing. For another, teachers of English have become increasingly concerned with the need to teach writing to students of science and technology, for whom ability in the spoken language may be secondary or even irrelevant. Finally, coinciding with the increased interest in written language by both linguists and ELT teachers has been a considerable growth in the study of language beyond the sentence, that is, in discourse.

The suggestions on writing that I will put forward in this book reflect these current concerns. My suggestions will also incorporate many current ideas which we may broadly term 'functional' or 'communicative'. In brief, a functional-communicative approach is concerned with the use of language for a purpose: to instruct, report, question, describe, comment upon, predict, and so on. But, as I hope will be clear, I do not advocate completely abandoning all of the principles and techniques which are traditionally part of the ELT teacher's repertoire of skills.

We will begin by looking at some of the characteristics of writing because, of course, we need to have some idea of what it is that we are teaching in order to be able to teach it.

3 WHAT IS WRITING LIKE?

So as to be able to understand some of the characteristics of writing, I will begin by contrasting two examples, the first of which may strike you as being familiar.

Example A
  She broke a glass. It began to snow. They liked grapes.
  You cut your foot. We came late. I lay on the beach.
  She taught French. The stream flowed to the lake. I knew her father. You lied to him.

Example B
  One day a friend came to Jason's house. The friend said: 'Please, Jason, will you help me to mend the roof of my house?'
  The friend and Jason went to a neighbour. The neighbour gave them a ladder and some tools. They took the ladder and the tools to the friend's house.
  Jason went up the ladder to mend the roof. He saw there were many holes in the roof, and in one of the holes he saw a nest. There was a mother bird and several baby birds in the nest.

Obviously, example A is simply a random collection of sentences. In other words, they are not interconnected in any way, save for the fact that they are all in the past tense. If the sentences strike you as being familiar, this is because they are an imitation of the kind of exercise which is still found in textbooks. In such exercises, the student is instructed to 'write the following sentences in the past tense'—or whatever tense is considered appropriate. Unfortunately, the sentences do not 'make sense' because, of course, each sentence appears to come from a different context, and as there are ten different sentences, so, too, there are probably ten different contexts.

As example B demonstrates, we do not usually write random collections of sentences. Instead, we usually write sentences in a connected fashion. How is this connection developed? The first and most obvious answer lies in the purpose of the communication. If, as in example B, our purpose is to tell a story of past events, there will be a common theme running through the sentences. There will also be a repetition of the names of people involved in the story. And, of course, there will be a logical order to the events reported. For instance, Jason could hardly see the birds in the nest until he had climbed the ladder, and he could not do that until he had obtained a ladder, and so on.

In addition to the functional and thematic link, there is an important grammatical link in example B. This is shown in the following pairs of sentences:

(1) A friend came to Jason's house. (2) The friend said . . .
(3) Jason went up the ladder to mend the roof. (4) He saw there . . .

A friend in sentence 1 has become *the* friend in sentence 2. This is because the friend has already been mentioned in the previous sentence. He has now become a particular friend. In sentence 4, Jason has become *he*. What we see here is the system of backward pointing reference of which 'backward pointing *the*' and the pronouns are very important components. In the sentences in example B, we can point back to the things or people to which such backward pointing items refer. In the sentences in example A, we cannot. If we cannot point back to something earlier in the text, the

What is Writing Like? 11

language becomes confusing. We say that it lacks *cohesion.* Cohesion is an important feature of all uses of language, as we can see in the next two examples, which contrast spoken and written versions of instructions on how to use a cassette recorder.

Example C is taken from the handbook to a Philips Cassette recorder, while example D is a transcript of a conversation in which I attempted to tell Marion Geddes how to use the same machine. Both examples share a common purpose—that is, to instruct in the use of the recorder—but they differ in medium, example C having been written to be read silently, while example D was originally spoken to be listened to.

Example C
Philips Cassette recorder:
RECORDING

—For recordings from the built-in microphone ensure that no equipment is connected to socket (1)
—For other recordings connect the separate microphone or the equipment from which you wish to record to socket (11)
—Insert a cassette
—Press record (2) and start key (4) at the same time
—To stop, press stop key (6)

Example D
Marion: Could you explain to me how to make a recording with this cassette recorder?
Ron: (er) Yes certainly. (um) First of all you (er) open the (er) place where the cassette goes, press down the button marked eject, then you put the cassette in and close the lid. (um) Then (um) to record you have to press down two buttons simultaneously, (er) the one marked rec for record and the one marked start. So you press those two down like that (Marion: Uhuh) and it starts recording (er) automatically. (um)
Marion: Ah it's automatic.
Ron: Oh yes (er) you don't need to adjust the volume because it has a special (er) microphone so that (er) it

	adjusts the level automatically.
Marion:	Oh I see.
Ron:	And (er) then when you want to stop you press the button marked stop, like that, that stops it, and then you rewind, press the rewind button, and wind forward you press the wind button (um) like that, and it winds forward and . . .
Marion:	That's going fast forward.
Ron:	That's going fast forward and (um) you keep the (er) button pressed down for as long as you want to wind it forward and then when you want to stop you just release the button like that.
Marion:	Ummm. And what if I want to record with a different microphone, not the built-in one here?
Ron:	There's a, a place, a socket here [Marion: Oh yes.] on the bottom left and you can put an outside microphone into that and record from another source.
Marion:	Oh thanks a lot.

Now, how do these texts differ? The first and most conspicuous difference is in length. The written text is very much briefer. Indeed, it is about one-fifth the length of the spoken version. The redundancy of the spoken text is most obvious in the section in which I begin 'First of all you (er) open the (er) place . . .' I take twenty-nine words to say what the written version does in three: 'Insert a cassette.' Clearly, then, writing is more concise than speech.

Writing is also visual. You can see the difference in length between the written instructions and the transcript. You can also see that the written version is set out in a particular way. There are well-established conventions of lay-out and presentation in the written instructions. These conventions serve an important purpose: they help the reader to comprehend the instructions. Imagine what the instructions would look like if they were written as a continuous paragraph, without indentations and separate lines for each step in the instruction sequence. Imagine, too, how much less easy they would be to follow. So, then, writing has visual means of organising the message.

What is Writing Like? 13

While reading the two texts you probably noticed another feature of the written version: it is more formal, less personal. In fact, there are no fewer than twelve occurrences of second person address (viz., *you*) in the spoken text, while there is only one in the written version. This is because the writer of the instructions was writing for an anonymous audience who were, of course, not present while he was writing. By contrast, while I was instructing Marion, she was actually present, and it is difficult to be impersonal with a friend who is there while you are talking. The face-to-face relationship of speaker and hearer also means that the speaker receives immediate feed-back from his audience to indicate understanding or the need for confirmation or clarification from the speaker, e.g. 'Oh I see' (showing understanding), 'That's going fast forward' (seeking confirmation). Such feed-back is not possible when we write.

The rather more formal style of the written text is also revealed in the choice of vocabulary. Whereas I used everyday terms like 'put in' and 'button', the written version includes somewhat more technical terms like 'insert' and 'key', although it is interesting to see that whereas I used 'simultaneously', the writer preferred 'at the same time', possibly in deference to his assumed audience. The need for clarity and ease of comprehension which motivated the choice of 'at the same time' has also made it necessary to refer to information outside the text itself. In the spoken version, this is shown by the use of such terms as 'like that' and 'here'. In the written version such information is indicated by the use of figures, e.g. (1), (11), which refer to labelled items in an accompanying illustration.

Finally, there is one feature of the written text which is unique to written instructions, and that is the omission of articles, e.g. 'Press record and start key'. A native English speaker who left out articles when telling someone how to use something would sound very odd. The omission of articles is common in written instructions of all kinds, though obviously it is not something that we would want to encourage in our learners for whom the inclusion of articles may still be a problem.

In this section we have looked at some of the formal features of written language. In the next section we will discuss some of the social roles of writing, and we will conclude by summarising the implications of both formal and social characteristics for the teaching of writing.

4 TYPES OF WRITING: INSTITUTIONAL AND PERSONAL

In their discussion of writing and reading in the context of using our native language, Davies and Widdowson (1974) draw a distinction between what they call Institutional and Personal writing. Institutional writing is the type of writing which we produce in our professional (or institutional) roles, such as that of school teacher, administrator, technician, and so on. What distinguishes such institutional roles from personal ones (such as that of friend, son, uncle, parent etc.) is that there are institutionalised conventions (or rules) as to how one behaves in relation to others who are part of the same institutional network. If, for instance, I am writing a letter as a customer to a business firm, there are conventions about what I will say and the way that I will say it. So long as I know what these conventions are, I am unlikely to make any gross errors in my communications with the firm. Similarly, the members of the company concerned will also play by the rules, and our business will proceed smoothly, efficiently and impersonally.

Business correspondence is an everyday example of institutional writing; but there are numerous others. Much of the reading and writing which most people do as part of their working lives—and here I include school children and students—falls into this institutional category. Textbooks and business memoranda, instructions and regulations, reports and proposals: all of these are examples of institutional writing which we all have to deal with from time to time in our working day. Because such institutional writing is so common, we are able to obtain numerous examples of it in the foreign or second language, and this has obvious advantages for student and language teacher alike. You may want to know where you can find such examples. If you have access to English-language material in such subjects as geography, history, general science, ecology, home economics, and so on, as well as newspapers, magazines and journals, you will have a valuable source of institutional writing from which to take examples for pedagogical purposes.

The same is not true of personal writing. Personal writing is of two main types: *personal letters* (or conversations on paper) and *creative writing*. Normally we write personal letters in our native language, unless we are corresponding with a pen friend with whom the only common language is a foreign one. Often, of course, teachers encourage such pen friendships as a means of providing a stimulus to writing in the foreign language concerned. But this is the problem: the pen friendship is a means to language improvement, whereas normally we write personal letters to people because we like and know them (or wish to know them and hopefully to like them).

Conversations on paper—like conversations in speech—between strangers are unlikely to prove very productive until both sides have something to say and a means of saying it. It may be even less easy for the student to say something on paper if he is being asked to reveal something of himself and his personality, which is what he is required to do in creative writing. Unfortunately, what is sometimes promoted as creative writing in the native language may be little more than a stringing together of items (often noun phrases) with much emphasis on feeling and little on logic. To transfer this to a foreign or second language is even less excusable. Besides, if people really do have something deeply personal to say, they are more likely to be able to say it (and to want to say it) in their own language.

I am not suggesting that we should completely outlaw personal writing from the ELT classroom, and you will find plenty of suggestions on linking writing exercises to such writing in Part Two. What I am pointing out is that personal writing is very much more difficult to teach and to learn because the conventions which govern interpersonal relationships (as opposed to institutional relationships) are so much more complex and varied than those which govern institutional roles. Even if our students do want to learn how to comport themselves in interpersonal interaction in both speaking and writing, there may well be a good case for giving them a basis in institutional language use first, for in learning to write institutional, referential, objective prose, appropriate to a professional or occupational role, they will be acquiring a foundation in the use of the forms and functions of language which will be enormously helpful when they embark on the less clearly mapped seas of interpersonal language use.

5 CONCLUSION: IMPLICATIONS FOR TEACHING WRITING

As was clear from examples A and B, writing involves more than just producing sentences. To be able to write a piece of prose, we must be able to write a connected series of sentences which are grammatically and logically linked. It is also necessary to be able to write appropriately for the kind of purpose and audience we have in mind, and it is in institutional writing that the guide-lines for appropriateness are most easily discovered, demonstrated and applied. We must also write in order to *communicate* something to our intended audience, and since this audience is not physically present, what we write must be as clear, precise and unambiguous as possible. In short, we must produce a piece of discourse which embodies correctness of form, appropriateness of style and unity of theme and topic. The implications of these requirements will be developed in the suggestions on writing in Part Two, beginning with a consideration of ways of prompting—or cueing—the student writer.

Part Two

6 TYPES OF WRITING EXERCISES: FALSE CUES

We have just seen how, when we write, we usually have a communicative purpose in mind and that we generally have something to write about (i.e. a topic). In other words, the writer himself specifies both purpose and topic. Such is rarely the case in the ELT classroom, and a major problem for the teacher lies in providing cues for student writing practice. What do I mean by a *cue*? Quite simply, a cue is a guide or example or stimulus which the student follows in order to produce a given type of writing. Various ways of doing this have been devised over the years, and I shall begin by reviewing two conventional types of writing exercises and pointing out their limitations as cueing devices. Then I shall take an example of what appears to be a good cueing procedure which, none the less, can give rise to unexpected problems. Finally, I shall outline some questions which we need to keep in mind when designing writing exercises and planning cueing devices for our students.

Writing exercises can be classified into two main groups: *sentence level reinforcement* exercises and *discourse level practice* exercises. The first type is usually linked to a particular language item, such as a tense or structure, which initially will tend to be presented and practised orally, often in dialogues and substitution drills. The written work is then intended to provide reinforcement of the language item in another medium. Here is an example of such a reinforcement exercise:

Examples: John is at home. John has gone home.
Write sentences in the same way. Use these items:
(1) cinema   (2) station   (3) meeting   (4) hospital   (5) his girl friend's   (6) church   (7) college   (8) disco   (9) airport   (10) hairdresser's

This sort of exercise can be criticised on a number of grounds. It is not, in any sense, communicative. It also provides the learner with a confusing contrast between two different tenses which are used in exactly the same context and, to all intents and purposes, with exactly the same meaning. The student might well ask: Why use two ways of saying the same thing when one will do? The items which the student is given as cues for further substitution practice are also confusing. Some would normally require the indefinite article—e.g. *a meeting, a disco*—others would usually be used with the definite article—e.g. *the hospital, the airport*—while some are generally used without an article at all (e.g. *church, college, home*). It would be tiresome to give further examples of reinforcement exercises of this type, particularly as most textbooks will provide a ready source of other instances. What you will not find in this book are exercises of this kind, because my main concern will be to suggest ways of practising discourse.

Discourse level practice exercises are not, of course, an innovation, though the way in which they are organised and presented may be. Here is an example of an exercise which, quite clearly, gives the student practice in writing a connected series of sentences as a way of reinforcing the use of the Simple Present tense. The student is instructed to put the verbs into the correct tense.

Tom usually (go) to work by bus. But he (go) to work by train yesterday. The bus usually (come) at 8 o'clock. He (get on) and generally he (stand). Sometimes he (see) a friend on the bus. He generally (arrive) at work at 8.45.

Types of Writing Exercises: False Cues 19

This kind of exercise, while incorporating interconnected sentences, does not really promote the practice of a contextualised piece of communication. Even so, it could be acceptable if it really did help the student to acquire control over the troublesome 3rd person singular Simple Present tense verb form (or *Base* + *s*). In fact, by presenting the learner with the infinitive (or *Base*) form of the verb, the exercise can only help to confuse and to undermine the learner's control over the very formal feature which he is supposed to be practising. An exercise such as this one might have some justification as a *test* item, to show whether or not the student could produce the correct verb form. But as a *practice* exercise it presents the learner with a testing task, and no practice exercise should place such traps in front of the student.

7 GOOD CUES: BAD RESULTS

I have suggested that many conventional exercise types do not provide a good cue for student writing practice. Yet, even what looks like being a good cueing device may not be very helpful to the student and it may even produce unfortunate results, as you can see from the passage below. (A correct version appears at the end of this section.)

First, the ingredients are weighing. Then they are mixing cullet, silica sand, soda ash, lime. Next the mixture is melting the glass melting tank. After then the glass is forming in the mould. Then the bottles are annealing the cooled bottles. Next they are inspecting in the rejects. Then they are packing in the box of cartons. After then they are storing. Finally they are distribution.

This passage, produced by a student in a test, contains several undesired errors, the most conspicuous of which is the use of the Present Progressive tense, active voice, instead of the Present Simple, passive voice. How did this error occur? If we look at the cue which the student was given, the cause of the error is obvious. The cue is shown in Figure 1.

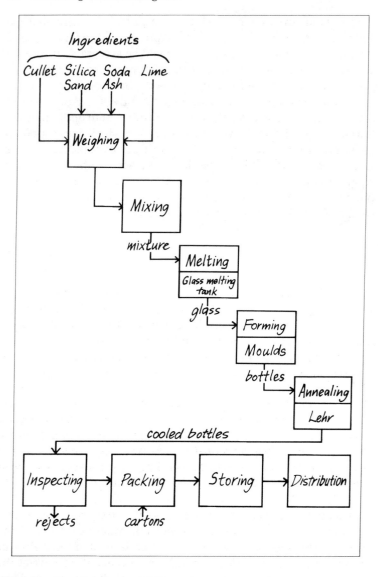

Figure 1   How Bottles are Made

It is fairly clear what has happened. The test item has required the student to make a grammatical transformation of a quite complex kind. She had first to remember that the Base + ing form of the verb (e.g. *weighing*) is the name of a step in the process. Then she had to remember the correct passive voice form for a written description (e.g. *is weighed*). This form consists of two parts: (1) a finite form of *be*, and (2) the past participle of the lexical verb. Next, the student had to rephrase the name of the process into the full passive voice form appropriate for a general description of the process. During this stage she may have recalled that the Base + ing form (i.e. *weighing*) can also be associated with the finite forms of *be* to make the verb phrase associated with the Present Progressive tense (e.g. *is weighing*). What she finally produced is, in fact, a sequence of verb phrases which (with the exception of *are distribution*), although formally correct, are entirely wrong in this particular context.

Obviously, this student was not yet ready to undertake the sort of transformation activity which this test demanded. And what is true of a test item is even more applicable to teaching, for the test item illustrates the ease with which the teacher can, quite unwittingly, induce errors in the learner by requiring him or her to perform such grammatical and/or morphological transformation exercises. Unfortunately, students are often given test items as prompts, with the kind of result that we have just seen. In a later section, we shall look at a way of teaching students to write descriptions of process, using flow diagrams as a cueing device, but avoiding the errors just discussed. In the meantime, we want to use the example we have just studied to ask some questions about writing exercises in general.

First, *will the cueing device confuse the student?* The kinds of confusions which may arise are not always as obvious as those which were demonstrated by the student whose work we have just looked at. Here is an example of a typical form of cue:

(1) *Did Michael go to the temple or not?*
(2) *Who did he see there?*
(3) *What was she doing?*

(4) *Did Michael speak to her?*
(5) *What did they find?*
(6) *Why were they afraid?*
(7) *How did they escape?*

This type of question and answer exercise is commonly linked to a reading passage and, indeed, the questions are a way of testing the student's understanding of the passage concerned. They also serve another purpose: the answers—'in full sentences'—are supposed to form a composition. But what is the student expected to do? In fact, he is being asked to carry out yet more complicated grammatical and morphological operations, not unlike those of our luckless student discussed earlier.

If we look at question 1, 'Did Michael go to the temple or not?', we see that the learner has to delete the 'dummy' helping verb *did*. Next, he has to change the Base form of the lexical (or main) verb into the correct Past tense form, *went*. Unfortunately, the student is confronted with the lexical verb in a form which may well confuse his possibly shaky command of the correct Past tense form. Since the meaning element is, in any case, contained in the lexical verb, it is all too likely that the writer will produce something like 'Michael go to the temple'. A similar confusion is also likely to occur with question 6, 'Why were they afraid?', in which the student has to shift the Past tense (*were*) from before the Subject to a place between the Subject (*they*) and the Complement (*afraid*).

There are ways of cueing the learner *without* asking questions, and some of these we will discuss in later sections. In the meantime, the example above may serve to illustrate the need to avoid cues which may confuse the learner by presenting him with a mixture of forms and a series of linguistic tasks which test him without, however, assisting him to write either accurately or communicatively.

Our next question is: *Will I want to use a good prompt for more than one purpose?* Most of us have a tendency to over-use a gimmick or a technique which we have found useful or successful. If, for instance, we have found a particular picture to be a good cue for teaching our students to write descriptions, we may decide to use the same picture to practise writing which includes other functions, such as narrative, as well as other grammatical elements, such as, for instance, conditionals. Quite apart from the boredom which is likely to result from over-use of the same visual aids, the learner will find it confusing if different uses of language are associated with one and the same visual cue. Normally, we use visuals to illustrate or demonstrate a particular area of meaning. The visual may also be a graphic substitute for physical response (as in following directions). If the learner finds that he is expected to make different linguistic responses to the same type of visual stimulus, he may become both confused and bored.

For instance, if we decide to use maps as a visual cue for writing, say, directions, we would be unwise to use maps as a prompt for writing descriptions, narratives and making suppositions. As it happens, maps are a very useful device for working on both directions and narrative, and we may want to use them for both. If we do, it would be a good idea to separate the two uses and possibly to introduce the second language function by using a different visual prompt, such as picture sequences rather than a map. Obviously we cannot always restrict our use of visual prompts in such a way that we use one cue for one purpose only. Even so, we should always weigh up the range of uses to which we may wish to put various cueing devices so as not to squander a good device on something for which it is not well suited.

Next, we come to our third question: *Will the cue be difficult to interpret?* If a picture is too detailed, it can be difficult for the learner to identify those elements which are crucial for the writing task in hand. Many published picture sets contain lots and lots of activities on the grounds that the teacher will be able to exploit them for teaching the 'commentary' function of language, such as 'In the front there is a boy. He is chasing a ball. Behind him his mother is sitting on a chair. She is knitting. Etc.' Teaching this commentary function of language is in any case of dubious value in writing; but the visual 'noisiness' of such a picture will be confusing for the learner and of little value.

At a more sophisticated level, graphs and tables may be useful as a means of cueing the writer. But, if the interpretation of the graph or table is in itself a demanding task, the learner may find himself facing a comprehension task of unreasonable and discouraging difficulty. This is not to say that we should not attempt to have our students interpret information presented in the form of visual displays since this is a skill that many of us have to perform every time we read a train timetable. What we must make sure of is that the interpretation task does not get in the way of our main purpose, which is to provide a useful and appropriate prompt for practising and developing writing skills.

Next, we come to our fourth question: *Does the student have the language needed to interpret the cue?* Even the most interesting and exciting visual cue is useless if the student does not have the language needed to describe or comment upon the item concerned. It is all too easy to find a visual display or even actual objects (i.e. *realia*) which appeal to us as teachers, and which we present to our students as a stimulus, only to find that we have forgotten to make sure that the students really have the language needed for the writing task we have in mind. The cue may, of course, be used as a means of demonstrating the need for certain language; but even here we must provide the student with a means of acquiring the language required for the writing exercise we want him or her to perform.

Finally, we should ask ourselves: *Is the cue a valid way of stimulating writing?* By this I mean, are we using a cue which naturally and realistically leads to the kind of writing we are using it for? For instance, if we take a piece of institutional writing, say a report on the production of a given product for the previous year, a tabulated set of figures would form a suitable and appropriate prompt. If, however, the writing task involves making predictions on the basis of past performance and embodying these predictions in a prospectus, line graphs which show more clearly the development of a trend over a given period of time would probably be a more effective means of providing the writer with information. Still on the institutional level, cues for writing a report of a business trip would appropriately be given in the form of an itinerary or a diary, in which the sequential organisation of the tour was clearly displayed together with other relevant information, such as the place and purpose of each visit, people seen and discussions held. Such a display of information would be more appropriate in this case than a picture sequence, since the form of cue I have suggested would be the kind of prompt which the business exccutive would actually have to use.

So, then, to summarise. First, make sure that the cues you use do not lead the student into making errors. Secondly, if you have a good cueing device, do not over-use it to the point of confusion and boredom. Thirdly, do not use cues which *you* cannot understand. Fourthly, make sure that the student has the language needed to interpret or make use of the cue. And finally, ensure that the cue is an authentic and valid way of providing the learner with information for the writing task you wish him to practise.

HOW BOTTLES ARE MADE: CORRECT VERSION

First the ingredients, cullet, silica sand, soda ash and lime, are weighed, and then they are mixed. Next, the mixture is melted in the glass melting tank. After this, the glass is formed in moulds. Then the bottles are annealed in the lehr. Next, the cooled bottles are inspected for rejects. Then the bottles are packed into cartons, and then they are stored. Finally, they are distributed.

8 REPORTING PAST EVENTS: NARRATIVE

In all cultures people report past events, and the receptive skills of listening and reading are well exercised in recreational contexts when we turn to the reading of fictitious or factual narrative. The ability to report events both in speech and writing is an important productive skill, and the teaching of narrative will occupy a significant place in most ELT programmes. In this section we are going to look at ways of teaching students to write narrative at both elementary and advanced levels, and with reference to both personal and institutional writing.

First, though, let us consider the following question: When, why and for whom do we write narrative? In personal language we write about events or activities in which we ourselves have taken part. Personal letters commonly contain such reports of the 'what we have been doing lately' variety. And, of course, no holiday postcard, letter to friends 'back home', or annual Christmas letter is complete without some such report, no matter how telegraphic in style it may be. Institutional writing also draws on this particular language function as the basis of reports on events and activities in such endeavours as business trips, surveys, meetings and research. Our primary intention in writing such reports, however simple in form they may be, is to provide friends or colleagues with a sequentially ordered account of events, though it is likely that we will also add description, explanation and commentary in order to provide colour, to give reasons for a particular outcome or consequence, and to express our own viewpoint or interpretation of what happened or what might have happened.

What does narrative consist of? Example B in Part One illustrates several key features. First, narrative is almost always in the *Past* tense. We can and do tell narratives in the Present Simple tense, but this is unusual and, except in rare instances, unacceptable. Secondly and above all, narrative is concerned with the *sequence* of happenings over a period of time. The fact that a particular sequence of events occurred in a particular order is what makes one story different from another. In some contexts, such as a report given by a witness to an accident or crime, failure to report the events in correct sequence can have serious consequences. Thirdly, narrative incorporates a number of language items which are important in showing *spatial* as well as sequential relationships. Finally, there are other features of narrative which we will want to incorporate once the three basic elements have been established. Some of these include statements of reason and cause and effect.

When teaching narrative at the elementary level, you will probably want to begin by establishing two things. First, you will want your students to associate the Past Simple tense with telling stories. Secondly, you will want to link the function of story telling to the concept of chronological sequence. To achieve these two aims, you need two things: (1) a list of regular Past Simple tense verbs, and (2) a picture sequence of about six related actions or events. Why regular verbs? The reason is simply this: in the early stages of learning, the student needs to see some pattern in language. If you present him with a series of mostly irregular Past Simple tense verbs during initial exposure to the tense, he will find it difficult to perceive any system. In other words, he will not be able to make any kind of generalisations about this aspect of the language. Obviously you will want him to meet and to learn the use of irregular verbs too; but it will be easier for him to do this if he can set them in a context of the regular Simple Past tense forms that he has already met. Furthermore, such controlled presentation of new items will help to ensure that an important objective is met, viz. that formal correctness is married to stylistic appropriateness.

Given our verb list and related picture sequence, we have a number of possible combinations open to us. These are summed up in Table 1.

Verbs	Pictures	Student Task
Correct sequence	Muddled sequence	To match muddled pictures to correct verb order
Muddled sequence	Correct sequence	To match muddled verbs to correct picture sequence
Muddled sequence	Muddled sequence	To work out correct sequence and match verbs to pictures

Table 1

How can we devise a lesson around these combinations? Here is one suggested order of activities. You can work out variations on this approach, given the other combinations listed in Table 1.

Lesson Plan

(1) Display the muddled picture sequence to Cl. (You may do this on the OHP.)
Ask SS to suggest an order for the events in the sequence.
Put the pictures into the correct order according to Cl suggestions.
Discuss reasons why the pictures must follow a given sequence.

(2) Present the sentences in muddled order. (You may also do this on the OHP, with each sentence written on a separate piece of acetate so that you can easily change the order and rearrange them into the correct sequence.)
Ask Cl to match the sentences to the picture sequence.
(Note: it is important that the pictures indicate direction clearly, as in climbing *up* and *down* the tree. When climbing up, Tim's head will be looking up, while in climbing down, he will be looking towards the ground. Similarly, when climbing up, his bag will be obviously empty, the reverse being true when he is climbing down. See Figure 2.)

(3) Write the correct sentence sequence in a table on the BB (or arrange the sentences on acetate slips in the correct order on the OHP). Table 2 shows the sentences in table form.

One day	Tim	discovered	some apples on a tree	.
	He	climbed	the tree	,
and	he	filled	his bag	.
Then	he	climbed	down the tree	.
Finally	he	carried	the apples to his house	.

Table 2

(4) Ask individual SS to read two of the sentences from the table. (It is important to have SS read more than one sentence at a

Reporting Past Events: Narrative 29

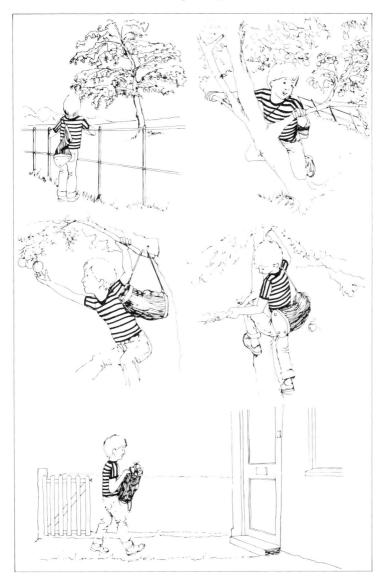

Figure 2 Narrative Picture Sequence

time, since you want them to get used to producing related sentences, not just individual ones.)
(5) Rub out all of the sentences, except for the verbs. Elicit complete sentences from SS, as in step 4.
(6) Remove the verb sequence and do as in step 5.
(7) Display the picture sequence in correct order.
Elicit the verbs from Cl.
Write them on BB (or OHP) under the appropriate picture.
(8) Have Cl write their own story in their workbooks, using the verbs and picture sequence as cues. Have them write their sentences in a table, as shown in Table 2, so as to emphasise sentence organisation and make it easy to check for the presence of Verbs, Subjects and Adverbials. Note also the punctuation column in the table.

In the above example you will have noticed a number of constraints. The vocabulary was limited, as was the total number of verbs. If you are teaching at an elementary level in particular, it is important to limit the quantity of new language which you present to your students at any one time. A good rule of thumb is to limit the number of new vocabulary items to five or six in any one lesson. Similarly, during the early stages of teaching narrative, restrict the number of actions in the story (and therefore the number of pictures) to about five or six. In any case, it is difficult to manipulate more than about eight pictures at a time, and the exercise becomes muddled and confusing if you use picture/action sequences involving ten or more items. Finally, throughout the exercise use the Past Simple tense form of the verb, since this is the form which we want students to learn.

The procedure of combining pictures and verbs or sentences can be employed with a number of variations. It is as well to vary the procedure because, of course, using exactly the same procedure for lessson after lesson is a sure way to kill student interest. Another variation can involve small group work, as outlined in the lesson plan given below.

Lesson Plan
(1) Issue a muddled picture sequence to Group A. Tell them to put the pictures in the correct order.
(2) Issue a muddled sentence sequence to Group B. Tell them to put the sentences in the correct order, independent of Group A.
(3) Call Group A to the front of the room. Tell them to hold up their pictures in the order they have decided upon. Ask Group B whether the picture sequence matches the order of their sentences. Encourage Cl discussion as to the correct order of events in the story.
(4) When an order is agreed, tell members of Group B to stand with their 'partner' in Group A. Ask individual SS to read sentences from the story.
(5) Tell groups to return to their seats, and then display the picture sequence at the front of the room, together with the verb cues (in the Past Simple tense), and tell Cl to write the story.

A further variation in this procedure involves the following activities:

Lesson Plan
(1) Issue sentences on flash cards to members of Cl.
(2) Call SS with cards to the front of the room, and tell them to stand in a line, displaying their sentences to the rest of Cl. Make sure that the SS are so arranged that the sentences appear in random order.
(3) Ask Cl to suggest the order in which the sentences should go. As suggestions are made, tell SS with cards to rearrange themselves. Eventually they should be standing in such a way that the sentences appear in correct sequence, from left to right.
(4) Ask Cl to read the sentences aloud. Then substitute the verbs for the full sentences, and have individual SS complete the sentences from the verb cues.
(5) As in the previous lesson plan.

This procedure can be enlivened by linking the story to a map on which a journey is plotted. The Cl can then use the map as a guide to the sequence of events in the story. If there are some 'traps' on the map (such as a one-way street system or two or more landmarks of the same kind, such as a church) the exercise can become very animated, and may provide useful incidental practice of such language functions as disagreeing and suggesting.

So far we have been considering matched picture/sentence sequences involving a fairly limited number of steps in the story. It is possible to use picture sequences of up to twenty or more pictures, provided the sequence is broken down into manageable units. Here is a suggested procedure:

Lesson Plan
(1) Divide a twenty-picture sequence into four groups of five pictures.
(2) Organise Cl into four groups, and issue each group with one of the five-picture sub-sequences.
(3) Tell each group that they are to work out the order of events for their own particular sequence, and that they are to suggest sentences for each event in the sequence. If you feel it is necessary, you can specify the first picture in each sub-sequence. Also, identify people in the pictures by name so as to avoid fruitless discussion on names.
(4) When each group has sorted the pictures into a sequence, they are to display them to the rest of Cl.
(5) Ask SS to suggest which of the four sub-sequences comes first in the overall sequence. Again, if you feel that it is necessary, you can tell Cl which set comes first.
(6) Organise the complete picture sequence and ask each group to give their sentences.
(7) Tell each group to write their part of the story. Students may write individually, though with group discussion about what to write.
(8) Tell groups to swap picture sub-sequences so that everyone can complete the rest of the story.

Another procedure involving an extended picture/sentence sequence can also be used.

Lesson Plan
(1) Divide the picture sequence into three or four sub-sequences, of about five or six pictures.
(2) Display the first group from the overall sequence in muddled order.
(3) Ask Cl to suggest an order and to say what happened in each picture. Once the pictures are in correct order, ask Cl to consider what might happen after the event depicted in the sequence. Write suggestions on BB or OHP.
(4) Display the next sub-sequence of pictures in random order. Are Cl suggestions from step 3 confirmed? What is the order of events?
(5) Continue as in steps 3 and 4.
(6) Display the third picture sub-sequence in correct order, and ask Cl to suggest sentences for each picture.
(7) Ask Cl to suggest how they think the story ended.
(8) Display correct picture sequence as a check.
(9) Tell Cl to write the story, using the verbs that have been suggested in the earlier steps of the lesson. The picture sequence, now complete, can be used as a cue. For the final pictures in the sequence (step 8), the SS can supply their own sentences, thus giving them the opportunity of providing something individual and original.

Obviously there are limits to the extent to which you can go on using such combinations of sentences matched with pictures. For one thing, there is a limit to the range of activities which can be presented in pictorial form. For another, older students and adults will tend to regard pictures as 'kids' stuff'. And, finally, none of us has unlimited resourcefulness and artistic skill. One solution to these difficulties is to use maps and itinerary tables, either by themselves or in combination.

How can we do this? Here is a suggested procedure, with a map

34 *Teaching Written English*

and an itinerary table, for use with intermediate-level students. A map (Figure 3) and an itinerary table (Table 3) are given here to illustrate the procedure.

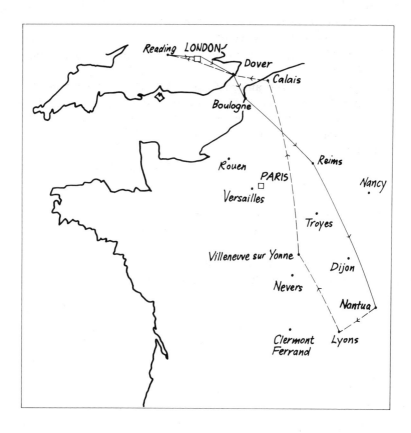

Figure 3 Map showing outward and homeward journeys in itinerary, Table 3

Lesson Plan
(1) Find or make up information on two similar journeys in which the travellers (A and B) follow routes which share certain places in common, but which differ in other respects.

Day and Date	from	to	miles	by
Monday 22 May	Reading	Dover	127	road and motorway
	Dover	Boulogne		hovercraft
	Boulogne	Reims	187	road
Tuesday 23 May	Reims	Nantua	297	road
Wednesday 7 June	Nantua	Lyons	60	road
Thursday 8 June	Lyons	Villeneuve sur Yonne	219	autoroute
Friday 9 June	Villeneuve sur Yonne	Calais	280	road and autoroute
Saturday 10 June	Calais	Dover		ferry
	Dover	Reading	127	road and motorway

Table 3

(2) Write the story of A's journey, or use an appropriate available text if one exists.
(3) Draw a simple map on which you mark the names of the places mentioned in both journeys.
(4) Make up an itinerary table for B's journey. The table will resemble the one shown here as Table 3.
(5) Prepare a blank itinerary table on the BB or OHP, together with a BB or OHP version of the map, with only places (but not routes) marked.
(6) Issue copies of the story of A's journey to Cl. (Note: the account of the journey could be in the form of a letter to a friend, or it could be a report of a journey of exploration such as would appear in a history or geography textbook. The nature of the account depends, of course, on the type of journey you select and the kind of reader for whom the narrative is intended.)
(7) Tell Cl to read the narrative and to underline the names of places.
(8) Elicit these names from SS and fill in the appropriate part of the blank itinerary on the BB or OHP.
(9) Ask individual SS to plot the route on the BB or OHP map.

(10) Elicit other items from Cl in order to complete the other parts of the itinerary table.
(11) Issue copies of an itinerary table for B's journey, in which all items are completed. Ask individual SS to plot this journey on the map. Remember to use a different colour of chalk or pen.
(12) Tell Cl to write an account of B's journey, using the report of A's journey as a model. Specify an intended reader for their composition.

As you can see, there is a significant reading comprehension element in this lesson. The provision of a model text is important as it shows the student what he should be aiming at in his own writing. The linking of reading and writing also provides for integration of these two skills, while the translation of information to and from graphic or table form practises information transfer skills in a way that is both interesting and useful.

As a variation on the above procedure, students can be provided with the following:

(1) The text of A's journey, though without its being identified as such.
(2) Itinerary tables for journeys by both A and B.
(3) A map, either with both journeys marked (but not identified), or with neither journey indicated.

The student has to read the text, compare the information with the itinerary table, and then identify the name of the person involved. Similarly, using this information, the student can then identify the route on the associated map. Finally, using the itinerary table and the map, the student can write a parallel account of the other journey.

In both procedures, the follow-up work can involve students in both personal and institutional writing, as required. They can, for instance, find out about journeys of exploration in their own region or journeys carried out by explorers from their own country. If, as is likely, the students themselves have travelled on a vacation, they can use the information as a basis for a narrative in the form of a letter or an article for the class or school magazine. Finally, if you are dealing with adults with more sophisticated requirements, the account of a journey could be written in the form of a report submitted to one's manager or head of department

In focusing on procedures, we have not so far considered the language involved in learning to write narrative beyond elementary level. Apart from learning to handle the Simple Past tense verb forms, students will also need to learn how to use adverbials of place, time and duration. Typically, a report of a journey will include such *adverbials* as the following:

at Paris	along Whitehall	for three days	at 11 o'clock
from Rome	down Regent Street	for twenty-four	at midnight
in London		hours	
through the Alps		from noon till	
across the Channel		midnight	
from London to New York			
by rail/car/air/ship/hovercraft/motorway			

There will also be *sequencers*:
 First
 Then
 After that
 Next
 Finally
 In the end.

In addition, there will be adverbials of *purpose* or *reason*:
 to see the El Dorado exhibition
 to do some shopping
 to visit the Louvre.

You will probably recognise some problem areas here. How many students 'arrive *to*' a place or stay there '*during* three days' or go there '*for doing* some shopping', and so on. Clearly, if you can, you will want to nip such errors in the bud by providing lots of practice of the correct forms. If you have a remedial teaching problem, then a lot of work will be needed to get rid of such unwanted forms. The kind of narrative practice I have described provides a very good context for such practice, and you can really focus on such problem items, using variations on the content and procedures I have suggested.

Finally, in the examples I have used I have not drawn on material belonging unambiguously to an institutional rather than personal context. My last example, given in full, intentionally links the writing of narrative with institutional writing, in this case from a geography textbook. The exercise was written for use with students in an ESL situation, in which they were using English as the medium of education at university level. The procedures followed are an elaboration of those already outlined for use at a less advanced level.

(1) Read the passage and:

    (i) put a box round the names of villages and settlements;
   (ii) ring the Base + ed verbs for each move of the Yega through their territory;
  (iii) number these verbs in sequence, beginning with (1);
  (iv) underline the words which tell when each move took place.

For instance, in paragraph two of the text your page will look like this:

By tradition, the Yega were sea people. This probably means that long ago they arrived (1) as migrants and originally spent most of their time . . .

(2) Now read the passage again, but this time

    (i) number the places on the map in the order (or sequence) in which the Yega moved there;

(ii) draw a line on the map indicating the path of Yega movements during the period discussed.

(3) Read the passage a third time and

(i) read for information needed to fill in the table Population Movements among the Yega;
(ii) complete the table.

(4) Write a summary of the text based on the information in the map and the table. Do not look back to the passage.

Reading Passage: The Yega

The Yega is a group of nearly 900 people living in sixteen settlements, on an area of about twelve square miles, on the north coast of Papua. They live on a gently sloping alluvial plain between Mt Lamington and the sea. During the last seventy years there have been a number of changes in the economic and social life of the Yega, and the economic changes in particular have brought about considerable changes in the pattern of settlement. Although most development has occurred in the last twenty years, there is evidence, supported by the oral traditions of Yega elders, to show that some evolution of settlement had occurred even before the first contact with white men.

By tradition, the Yega were sea people. This probably means that long ago they arrived as migrants and originally spent most of their time aboard their canoes and that they lived mainly upon seafood. They settled first on three small islands, Baroda Deuga, about half a mile north-east of Wasusu. These islands are composed entirely of coarse coral sand and lumps of dead coral. Although there are mangrove trees on the islands, there is no possibility of growing food crops there, and this would have been true in earlier times.

At some time well before the arrival of white men, the Yega moved from Baroda Deuga and founded a village, Basabuga, on the eastern shore of Wasusu Point. In Basabuga each clan was allocated a specified area in which family heads built their homes. Probably there were only three original clans, but these were joined at intervals by ancestors of the other five clans who make up the Yega parish. Basabuga is on an ideal defensive site, protected on the landward side by mangrove swamps to the south-east, and on the south-western side by swamp-filled depressions running parallel to the beach. The sea provided an escape route to the north.

Up to 1910 when the first school was begun at Wasusu Point, some clans moved eastward or westward and settled in other coastal villages, such as Tarebosusu and Kanunje. The main reason for the dispersal of clans from Basabuga was probably population pressure; but the enforced cessation of interparish warfare undoubtedly contributed. The movement westward along the beach from Tarebosusu to Beporo and Gona continued until about 1930. People were encouraged to move by the increasing effectiveness of government control and by the establishment at Gona Mission of a school and hospital staffed by Europeans. The new coastal village sites also reduced walking time to the gardens.

The war of 1939-45 affected the Yega in several important ways. Their territory became one of the major battlefields of the Pacific War. Every person migrated from the area. Most of the able-bodied men went away to serve in the army or labour corps, while the women and children shifted to another Anglican mission about thirty miles to the north.

When they returned at the end of the war, they found everything destroyed. They were paid some compensation. Meanwhile, the war had brought with it new experiences and changes in attitudes among the younger men. In addition, the transfer of administrative headquarters from Buna to Higatutu resulted in the construction of a major road to the port of Cape Killerton, and this brought the Yega into closer touch with the outside world than ever before. As a result, between 1945 and 1950, about twenty families left their re-built villages between Gona and Basabuga and they moved east to found the new village of Surilai at Cape Killerton. Men living at Surilai have since found regular employment on the government wharf at Cape Killerton.

Since 1960, seven new inland villages have been established along the road leading from Gona Mission to the town of

Reporting Past Events: Narrative 41

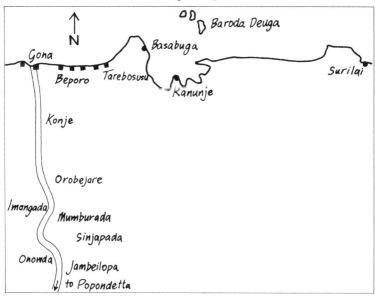

Figure 4   Settlement Patterns of the Yega

Population Movements among the Yega

Time	Moved from	To	Reasons for Moving
Pre European		Basabuga	
1930			
	all villages		
			the end of the war
		inland villages	

Table 4

Popondetta. This movement inland from the coast was initiated by the development of a cocoa-planting project. As the cocoa blocks were a long walk from their homes in Beporo village, many people moved inland, and by 1964, over half the Yega population was living in the new villages to the south of Gona and Beporo. (Adapted from R. B. Dakeyne, *Village and Town in New Guinea*. Longman.)

NARRATIVE: SUMMARY

In teaching the writing of narrative for both personal and institutional uses:

(1) Focus on chronological sequence, that is the order of events or activities.
(2) Use cueing devices which will exemplify order, such as picture sequences and maps and itinerary tables of journeys.
(3) Link the cueing devices to a 'thinking' task, such as working out the order of events, or transferring verbal information to visual form, or interpreting visual information in verbal form.
(4) Avoid using questions and answers as a means of eliciting narrative.

9 DESCRIBING OBJECTS

We will now turn to our second major language function: description. It is important to distinguish between description and narration, although sometimes the two are classed together under some such heading as 'reporting' or even simply 'describing'. As we have already seen, narration involves the concept of sequence, and not just any old sequence, but a particular order of events over time. There is, in short, a necessary logic to narration. With description, however, there is no hard and fast logical constraint on the organisation of what we write. There is, as we shall shortly see, a constraint on the kinds of thing we write about in a description;

but there is no invariable, fixed order in which we should write about them.

A second point is that a lot of description involves the use of the Present Simple tense, whereas narrative typically involves the Past Simple. Clearly, then, description provides us with a good context in which to present and practise the use of the Present Simple tense. But that is not all. In narrative it is *activities* which are important; in description it is *things*. And in describing things we are usually more concerned with the *noun* rather than the verb phrase. Thus, description gives us a reason for teaching features of the noun phrase which, while occurring in other uses of the language, are of particular importance and frequency in describing things, people and places.

We shall begin by looking at a description of an object.

Here are the hammock's vital statistics. It is free-standing, easily and quickly assembled and dismantled. The 'weather-sealed' frame may be left out in the open, and the fabric taken indoors after use. The fabric is of non-fading, red, green, blue and white-striped, rot-proof material, and the seams are reinforced with rot-proof thread. The overall length of the tubular frame is 7ft 10in. The hammock itself is 6ft long and 20in wide at the head, 22in wide at the foot. The ropes are of strong rot-proof polypropylene. The hammock is 2ft above the ground and it has been tested to carry up to 250lb weight. It is easily transportable in a car as the overall length of the dismantled frame is only 3ft and the whole pack weighs about 15lb.

This description gives us the following information on the object concerned:

Name of object
Size
Weight
Materials
Colour
Other features

The text was taken from a 'special offer' article in *The Times*, and is an example of institutional writing. It exemplifies a context in which we write (and read) such descriptions. Basically, the article is intended to inform the interested reader about the hammock, giving information which can only be presented verbally. In fact, the same information could be produced in tabulated form as a specification sheet or entry in a manufacturer's catalogue, and as we shall see, such a summary can be used for exercises connecting both reading and writing descriptions of this type. The important point is that a description of an object is written (or spoken) when the reader/hearer cannot be fully informed by an illustration alone.

This gives us a purpose for writing such descriptions, and as we have just seen, we now have the main topic headings for organising a description. What we now need to do is to see how we can present and practise writing descriptions of objects in the ELT class. I will assume, for the purposes of this example, that the students have either been introduced to the following language items or that some of them will in fact be presented in the lessons dealing with description:

Language items

Adjectives of colour and shape
Vocabulary of measurement, both size and weight
is and *has* (for obvious reasons these items should be presented in separate lessons)
Sentence pattern: Subject + Verb (be) + Complement
                  Subject + Verb (have) + Object
a + singular count noun
zero article + non-count noun

The procedure to be followed involves the use of a set of pictures of objects (or realia) together with three written texts. The students are presented with one of the texts as a reading comprehension exercise and they are asked to match the text with the appropriate object. The combination of elements is summarised in Table 5.

Describing Objects 45

Object	Colour	Size	Price	Place of Origin
a	✓	✗	✓	✗
b	✗	✓	✗	✓
c	✗	✗	✓	✓

Table 5

If we have three of the same type of object (e.g. a car) we can vary their characteristics by only one feature at a time so that the objects will be alike in two respects but different in one; and so on. This means that the students will have to match the descriptions quite carefully with the array of objects. The matching procedure which forms the comprehension task has real-life parallels: we describe objects in order to discriminate them from others of the same kind. There is, thus, an important communicative element in this part of the exercise.

Here is a brief example. First, collect some coloured pictures of motorcars. Such pictures are easily obtained, either from manufacturer's brochures, or from magazines. They can be pasted on to cardboard and re-used. Provide students with five or six such pictures and three reading texts, of which the following is an example:

Passage
This car is expensive. It has a big
motor and it is fast. It has five seats
and a large boot. It is from Germany.

The picture cards can be set out as shown in Figure 5.

The students match the descriptions to the pictures. Obviously some of the cars illustrated will share many characteristics in the descriptions so as to make the matching task more challenging. Once the students have succeeded in matching the text to the

Price: £3,800
Motor: 1442 cc
Top Speed: 95 m.p.h.
Seats: 5
Boot: 12·4 cu ft
Country: Britain
Name: Talbot Alpine GLS

Figure 5

illustrations, they can then write three parallel descriptions of their own, based on the remaining pictures. If they are working in groups of four or five, the groups can then swap their sets of pictures and the descriptions that they have written. Each group then has to match the new pictures and texts as in the first stage of the lesson.

In the exploitation stage of such work, reference can be made to objects in the students' own environment. There must, of course, be a purpose to this so as to avoid merely writing descriptions for the sake of writing them. There are several contexts in which descriptions of objects occur. We have already seen one—a newspaper article. In the commercial world such descriptions form part of sales literature, usually with praise of the object being part of the message. In geography textbooks—particularly those sections which describe the material culture of a human group—artefacts are commonly described. Any one of these institutional types of writing can be practised, and useful links can be made with other subjects, such as geography, home economics, and manual crafts.

In the work outlined above, I made no mention of language as such. At an elementary level, particularly with younger learners, overt discussion of features of the language is not recommended, except in the most concrete terms. For instance, students may be asked to point out what the verbs have in common—only the term 'verb' need not be used since pointing to the words in question should suffice. Similarly, many of the noun phrases will share a common feature, such as the presence of a + noun. Students can be asked to find the common feature and to make generalisations based on their discovery. In other words, they can be encouraged to make simple grammatical generalisations expressed in their own terms.

At a more advanced level, grammatical discussion can be linked to functional features of the language used in describing objects. There is an important distinction in meaning between modifiers that I will call *epithets* (large, splendid, graceful, attractive) and those which can be called *classifiers* (all colour terms, wooden, steel, plastic, striped, Elizabethan, rot-proof etc.). Epithets are terms which are subjective in meaning, for what is large, splendid or attractive is relative to the viewpoint of the individual—and viewpoints vary. However, whether something is wooden, steel, plastic or Elizabethan is not a matter of opinion, for there are objective grounds for classifying something as being one or the other.

This distinction in types of modifier can be related to different types and functions of writing. The advertiser, who seeks to praise the object he wants to sell, will tend to use epithets, while the would-be purchaser may be more interested in those qualities indicated by classifiers. So, in our first phase we could use some advertising texts and ask our students to distinguish between those features which are open to subjective evaluation and those which are not. We can then relate the distinction to the two types of modifiers: epithets and classifiers. Production exercises can make use of this distinction by requiring the students to write descriptions for a different purpose: one description intended to praise and persuade, that is to advertise; the other intended to inform a prospective customer of the purely objective attributes of the same item. The exercise also allows us the opportunity of introducing other stylistic features, such as lay-out, appropriate to the differing purposes of the writing concerned.

Although we have looked at general procedures, there still remains the problem of how to cue the writer. There are three possibilities. First, we can use a specification table like the one given in Table 6.

Object	a T'ang horse
Material	pottery
Age	1,000 to 1,300 years
Original function	a funerary figure
Height	72 cm
Colour	Parts
orange-brown	body
cream	mane
cream	tail
green-brown	saddle
Price	£68,000
Buyer	Eskenazi, the London dealer

Table 6

The information on this splendid object was taken from a report in *The Times* from their Sale Room Correspondent, and the table, with only the headings provided, was used in conjunction with the text in a comprehension exercise with a group of adult students. Then, using the table which they had completed, they wrote their own descriptions as for a catalogue entry. Basically, the same type of table can be used, with some variation in headings and content, for almost any object, and the student can use the information from the table as a basis for his own written text. Table 7 provides another example. This is part of an exercise in which the student practises writing a description of an object in a piece of personal writing. The instructions to the student are also given here.

You have a friend who will soon have a special birthday party. Another friend has written to ask you what you are going to give to your mutual friend. Reply to your friend's inquiry by describing the gift, the specification of which is given in Table 7.

name	Florentine box
material	Fine leather
measurements	length: 6 in width: 4 in depth: 2¼ in
features	Exterior: fine leather with gold decoration Inside: velvet
function	for keeping jewellery

Table 7

The second type of cue is a purely visual one, in which an illustration is used. The illustration can be either labelled or unlabelled, depending on the familiarity of the students with the type of object concerned. Advertisements (such as the Rollei advertisement shown in Figure 6) or illustrations from instruction booklets provide a useful source of visual cues.

Finally, the third type of cue is, of course, a real object. As with using pictures, care needs to be taken when using realia. If the students do not have the necessary vocabulary, they will not be able to describe the object, so although realia may provide a glamorous focus for the writing class, remember that you will have to feed in the necessary vocabulary to enable your students to write.

50 *Teaching Written English*

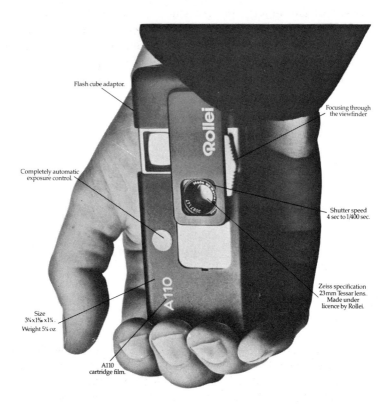

Figure 6

Describing Objects 51

In our discussion of describing things, we have been concerned with the *physical attributes* of an object: size, colour, materials etc. There is another important feature and that is the *use* or *function* of an object. A description of how an object works will usually be part of its description, and it may also be part of a set of instructions on how to use a piece of equipment. Although such descriptions belong in a technical or semi-technical field, there is no need to feel intimidated because most of us today have an extensive understanding of semi-technical literature, such as we find in the handbooks accompanying even domestic equipment such as washing machines and vacuum cleaners.

Descriptions which deal with what something looks like do not, as I mentioned earlier, follow any particular logic in their organisation. There is not, for instance, any rule which states that we should deal with colour first, and then size, and then material, and so on. When, however, we come to describing how something works, the organisation of our description is determined by the sequence of actions in the operation of the equipment. Here is a description of how a piston pump works, and this follows a logical sequence:

A piston pump consists of a cylinder, a piston connected to a handle, an inlet valve and an outlet check valve. The piston is pushed downwards to force air out through the outlet valve. Then the piston is pushed upwards to suck air in through the inlet valve. On the return downward stroke, the inlet check valve is forced against the piston wall, thus preventing any air from escaping, while the outlet check valve opens to allow the air to flow through the connecting tube. Pumping is continued by moving the piston up and down in the cylinder.

Clearly, here we must begin our description either at the upward or downward stroke of the piston, and continue the description through a complete cycle in the pumping process. Obviously the description and the related cycle of activities should be illustrated, either graphically or by demonstration with realia. Furthermore, the sequence and logic signals used in such a description—*then, thus, while*—and the adverbials of manner—*by moving*—will also have to be pointed out and practised.

One procedure to teach writing such a description involves displaying diagrams in which the action sequence is illustrated. Then students are issued with the text, but with the sentences in random order. This is most easily done by having each sentence on a separate slip of paper so that students can easily sort the sentences into the correct order as they work. The students then have to put the muddled slips into the correct sequence according to the diagrams they have studied. After this, you can elicit the correct sequence from the class, and write the sentences on the blackboard or OHP, like this:

	The piston	is pushed	downwards	to force air through the inlet valve.
Then	the piston	is pulled	upwards	to suck air in through the inlet valve.

Using these sentences as a cue, ask individuals round the class to describe the operation of the pump. Then successively rub out or cover sections of each sentence, beginning with the element on the right (the adverbials) and moving left till eventually all the sentences have been obliterated. At each successive stage, the students are asked to produce more and more of the sentences. The final stage sees them writing the description, using only the labelled diagrams as a prompt. For follow-up work, the students work from illustrations or diagrams of equipment embodying a similar cyclical process, e.g. a water pump, a sewing machine, an internal combustion engine, a coffee percolator. In this phase, the students apply the points which they practised in the earlier exercises.

DESCRIBING OBJECTS: SUMMARY

In teaching the writing of descriptions of objects:

(1) Give greatest attention to the noun phrase, as this provides most of the important information in such descriptions.

(2) Link the writing task to identification and sorting activities using pictures or realia.
(3) Make sure that your students have the language items needed in order to write the description that you set them.
(4) Choose personal or institutional contexts in accordance with the students' requirements and abilities.

10 DESCRIBING PEOPLE

When and how do we describe people? As far as simple, physical description is concerned—that is describing what someone looks like—we probably do not produce such descriptions very much in writing, although a description of someone's appearance may be part of a more comprehensive description which includes information on their behaviour, possessions and attitudes. In institutional writing, such descriptions may be found in newspaper and magazine articles and, with some important additional features, in some types of advertisement and publications dealing with occupational roles and requirements.

What form do such descriptions take? Let us look at this excerpt from a *Sunday Times* article on a journey across the Atlantic by Concorde. We shall study the second paragraph of the article, which describes Chris Morley, Concorde captain.

He is one of the original seven British Airways Concorde pilots, and only the week before he has taken Mr Callaghan to Washington to meet President Carter. He is Central Casting's idea of a senior airline captain, 47, glamorously grey, firm of jaw, calm of voice, with a lean athletic build and a mien of command and reassurance. He earns more than £16,000 a year which still puts him low in the league in comparison with foreign captains. He has four children, a pretty wife, a spacious house, and an 11-year-old Renault 16, which he now gets into to drive to Heathrow.

This paragraph gives us the information summarised in Table 8.

Job	British Airways Concorde pilot
Age	47
Appearance	glamorously grey, firm of jaw, lean athletic build
Manner	calm of voice, mien of command and reassurance
Salary	£16,000 + per year
Family	Wife, four children
Possessions	a spacious house, an 11-year-old Renault 16

Table 8

The paragraph makes use of two sentence patterns, shown in Table 9.

Subject	Verb	Complement
He	is	one of the original seven BA Concorde pilots.
Subject	Verb	Object
He	has	four children.

Table 9

And the predominant verb form throughout is the troublesome Base + s, while, with one exception—*has taken*—the tense is the Simple Present, though in the article it is used to tell a narrative.

These, then, are some of the basic elements in a description of a person. The problem now is how to present and practise these. At an elementary level essentially the same elements can be presented as part of listening and reading comprehension exercises, with the students checking off or entering items in a table, like Table 10.

Name	Age	Eye Colour	Hair Colour	Height	Clothes
Charles Wood		blue			a sweater and jeans
Carmen de Silva	30		long black		
Jenny Jones				5 ft 4 in	

Table 10

Some of the items are given, the rest have to be completed by the students as they listen or read. Using the completed table, students can then write a description following the model which they have heard or which they have read, thus:

Charles Wood is 22. He has blue eyes and short blonde hair. He is tall. He wears a sweater and jeans.

As yet, there has been minimal communication in such an exercise. In order to link the receptive and productive aspects of description to a communicative purpose, we can provide a selection of pictures (either simple sketches or photographs of real people). The task for the students is to sort out the illustrations according to the descriptions which they read and write. To make the task more challenging, it is a good idea to have several more pictures than descriptions, and to make sure that some people depicted share some things in common. (Cf. a similar procedure in Section 9 dealing with 'Describing Objects'.) The students' task involves intellectual as well as linguistic skills, while at the same time practising the function of description in an approximation to authentic use.

Providing a challenge or a puzzle element, even when teaching writing, is a good idea both to maintain a communicative purpose in using English and to sustain interest and motivation. The same principle can be applied at a slightly more advanced level when we wish to introduce new information within the context of describing people. In the *Sunday Times* description, the writer told us about Captain Morley's *manner* as well as his appearance. In general, when we describe someone, we mention those features of appearance and personality which are most striking to the observer. Indeed, a description is concerned with what makes a person *different* from others rather than in giving a list of what makes him similar. Obviously, people tend to share many features, but it is the combination of characteristics which makes one person different from another.

The combination of shared and unique features and characteristics which makes up an individual's identity can be displayed in tabulated form and this is a good way of demonstrating both sameness and difference. The table can be linked to a model text in which students are shown the sort of description which they should write. Care must be taken with the table, however, since it is all too easy for students to use it to write something like this:

> *Tim Elliot's age is 25. His wife is typist. He has own business. His car is Chrysler Horizon. His interests are fishing and gardening. Etc., etc.*

To help overcome this tendency simply to use mostly the verb *be* (which is, of course, very frequently used in description), students can be instructed to write the verbs from the model text in appropriate parts of the table. The text itself should leave something open to the students by omitting the name of the subject of the description. This means that they have to match the information in the description with that given in the table. So, the text could look something like this:

> *X is a football player. He plays for the Ambridge Colts. He is — years old and he is married. His wife's name is — and she is —. X and his wife live in —. He drives — and he enjoys fishing and gardening. At home he helps with the children. He reads the* Guardian.

And the table could look like Table 11.

Once students have identified the subject of the description, using the clues in the text, they can complete the blank spaces before writing parallel descriptions of their own, using the information in the table. After writing one description following very closely the organisation of the model, pupils can then be encouraged to vary the order of sentences (and information). They can also omit the name of the subject of the description (as in the original text) and exchange their descriptions and then guess the identity of the subject, using the information in the table as a guide. Finally—and this always proves to be an amusing task for adults and children alike—they can write anonymous descriptions of members of the class, or a pop star, or someone well known in the

Verbs	Bill Hardcastle	Tim Elliot	Charles Johnson
is	a football player	a football player	a racing driver
plays for drives for	Ambridge Colts	Ambridge Colts	Team Lotus
is	25	27	31
is	Wife: Sandra a typist	Wife: Liz a teacher	not married
live	a flat	a house	a flat
drives	a Capri	a Chrysler Alpine	a Lotus Elan
enjoys	fishing and golf	fishing and gardening	skiing and sailing
helps with	shopping	the childrem	—

Table 11

local community. A lot of amusement can be derived from having each student read aloud his description, the rest of the class then attempting to guess the subject of the text. Similar descriptions for a 'guess who?' competition could also be written for the school magazine, if one exists.

In the above examples, we have taken a set of categories for description, varied the information in each category, and used it as a basis for an identification task. But what of the context in which such descriptions may occur? A description of individuals, particularly as members of a family, obviously has a restricted range of contexts, of which the pen-friend letter is perhaps the most hackneyed. A more valid context, and one which will provide a wider range of exploitation, is that of the geography or social studies textbook or a handbook on a town or country, which takes a 'typical' family or families as a vehicle or means of providing information about the way of life of the place concerned.

We can use a family tree as the visual cue for such a description. Here the combination of items is as follows:

A text describing one part of the family tree.
A half-completed family tree, the blank half corresponding to

the text, the completed half providing a cue for the follow-up writing task.

The procedure is as follows:
(1) Tell Cl to read the description of the 'X' family. (See example in exercise below. Note that the names of the people are given in the text so that the students have to work out the identity of individuals by comparing the descriptions with the information given in the blank half of the family tree, Figure 7. The blank half shows men, women, children and ages, but not names.)
(2) Tell Cl to compare the description with the family tree.
(3) Tell them to fill in the blank names on the family tree.
(4) Tell Cl to write a parallel description based on the completed half of the tree.
(5) For follow-up, SS are to write a description of their own families, with associated family trees.

Reading Passage

Philip Sinclair is a journalist. He is in his late twenties, and he is one of five children of Lewis and Margaret Sinclair. Philip's wife, Jane, is also in her late twenties, and she and Philip have two children: Simon, aged 7, and Celia, aged 5. Philip has two brothers and two sisters. His brother Damien is a year younger than Philip. Damien is a travel agent. Philip's younger brother, Matthew, is in his late teens and like Damien, he is not married. Philip's older sister, Louise, is in her mid-twenties, and she is married to Adrian Mountford. Louise and Adrian have three children: Clare and Stephen, twins aged 6, and Rosemary, aged 4. Philip's younger sister, Madeline, is in her early twenties. She is not married. Philip's father, Lewis, is in his mid-fifties and he is a bank manager. Philip's mother, Margaret, is a year younger than her husband.

All of the descriptions which we have looked at so far have been concerned with who people are (i.e. relationships), what they look like (appearance), and how they behave (manner). When we describe people, particularly in an institutional context when giving accounts of a way of life and a culture, we become concerned with roles and routines. In our daily lives we all perform different roles in relation to other people in our social world. As we carry out our daily routines we shift from one role to another. Besides making sense, it also adds interest, if we deal with 'a day in the life of' someone by organising the description not only in terms of the repeated activities which form part of a routine, but also by seeing how these are classified according to the different roles a person carries out in his or her 'typical' day. This approach also gives us the opportunity of providing repeated practice of the Base + s verb form of the Present Simple tense, while at the same time introducing another important language item, the adverbials of frequency.

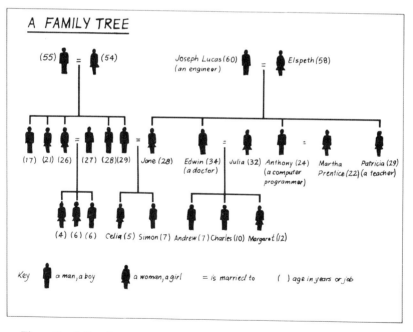

Figure 7 A Family Tree (R. V. White, *Functional English* (Nelson 1979))

We can present information to our students in the form of a text which describes a daily routine. The students' task is to abstract information from the text and to organise it into a timetable which distinguishes between one role and another, as shown in Table 12.

Role: Son	Student	Friend
gets up does paper round*		
	arrives at school attends classes	
		plays football visits friends' homes
arrives home		
	does homework	

*Doing a paper round involves delivering newspapers to people's houses.

Table 12

Parallel information can be given for a counterpart production exercise, leading on to students' accounts of the lives, roles and routines of members of their community.

We have now moved into the field of job description, which is of some importance in institutional writing, particularly in the context of commercial or professional occupations. A job description is concerned not so much with the individual person as with the activities which someone performs when he or she is employed in a particular job. Here is an example taken from a publication in the series on careers, published by the Careers and Occupational Information Centre of the Employment Service Agency.

The day's routine
Roger's day begins at 8 o'clock with a quick inspection of the sections he is responsible for. He sees that none of the previous day's output 'looks wrong', and checks the date codes which are printed on all packages to make sure nothing in stock is older than the previous day. Then he holds the daily morning conference with his inspectors, who report on quality checks made

on raw materials to be used during the day, on weight checks, airtight seal checks, and so on of the previous day's production.

This type of job description can provide a basis for reading and writing work, with focus on what is done in a particular job. We can begin by giving students some descriptions of what certain people do in each job, but with the information in random or scrambled order. The students' task is to put the items into correct order and to write them out as complete descriptions. Here are two examples. In the first the information is in correct order, in the other it is in random order.

Examples

A pilot	*An air hostess*
prepares the flight plan	*shows them to their seats*
examines loading documents	*checks the food and drink*
checks the aircraft controls	*helps passengers off the aircraft*
starts the engines	*welcomes passengers on board*
flies the aircraft	*serves food and drink*
lands it at its destination	*makes in-flight announcements*

The unscrambling exercise involves a reading comprehension element, but this is not simply an optional extra, for writing involves the ability to organise logically and coherently. In the example above, the idea of chronological sequence within a routine is implicit, and students must be able to apply the same concept in writing job descriptions of their own. This stage can involve a 'research' element in situations where this is either possible or appropriate, in which the eventual description may be based on the answers to a questionnaire devised by the class. Of course, this does involve the use of another language function, viz. questioning, but it does also have the advantage of providing an opportunity to write questions and answers in an authentic context. (Cf. section 14 on 'Questions and Answers'.)

Even if questioning people about their jobs is not possible, students can work out from observation and experience the main activities of the jobs concerned. This can be done as small group work, each group having a different job to work on. The job description can then be presented either as a group assignment or as individual written work. There are also other possibilities for extending the work on job descriptions, and even of linking it to a simulation study. For example, we can devise a situation in which an organisation is in the process of being established, and members of the management have to agree on job specifications for a number of new posts. The jobs will, of course, be related to the structure and functions of the organisation concerned, and it may be important that the job descriptions are such that overlapping of work or competition between posts is avoided. The writing of the job descriptions, therefore, becomes a challenge to the 'management' team. If several teams in the class work on the same job descriptions, some useful comparisons and discussion can be generated when each team presents its solutions in the form of the written job descriptions it has devised.

In all of these job descriptions we have been concerned with what people regularly or actually do or are expected to do as part of their jobs. Another topic is that which specifies requirements for a given job. Such a specification may be part of an advertisement, thus:

To succeed in this challenging appointment, you must have at least three years' sales management experience in electronic components, communications or industrial electronics. An appropriate degree or relevant professional qualification is essential. Preferably aged 35-40, male or female, you must be a self-motivating, innovative and energetic leader.

Or it may be in a careers advisory publication, such as those published by the UK Employment Service Agency.

Women are normally recruited as air stewardesses or hostesses between the ages of 20 and 27. They must be unmarried, in good health with a well-proportioned figure, good appearance and carriage and an easy, confident manner. A sound general education is essential and it is definitely an advantage if not

essential to have 'O' level passes.
[Note: 'O' level passes are passes in the 'Ordinary' level Certificate of Education Examination at secondary school. There is also an 'A' or Advanced Level.]

These requirements are specified using *must*, and so we have a useful context for presenting and practising this particular modal verb. It will be advisable, of course, to separate the presentation of job descriptions with *must* from those descriptions and writing exercises in which the Base + s form of the Simple Present tense has been stressed. This new type of job description also provides us with a good context for distinguishing between qualifications which are essential and those which are desirable but not essential (such as 'O' level passes). The content of the descriptions can range from jobs which are within the scope of knowledge and interests of school students (e.g. nurse, teacher, shop assistant, secretary) to those which are restricted to special groups of learners (e.g. business executive, technician).

Provided that we give them examples of descriptions of requirements for a job, as in texts like those quoted above, devising job specifications is a task which the students can undertake themselves. The job specification may be summarised in note form, similar to that set up for the specification of an object. Table 13 provides an example.

Job	air hostess
Sex	female
Marital status	single
Health	good
Appearance	well-proportioned figure, good carriage
Manner	easy, confident
Education	'O' level advantageous

Table 13

The qualifications can be further sub-divided into those which are essential (you *must* have them) and those which are advantageous or desirable (you *should* have them), thus:

Must have/be
single
a sound general education

Should have/be
'O' level passes

Using specification lists like these as examples and as cues for writing parallel descriptions of their own, students can work out similar specifications for other jobs. It might be interesting to discover what they regard as being essential characteristics for being a good teacher!

DESCRIBING PEOPLE: SUMMARY

In teaching the writing of descriptions of people:

(1) Organise the descriptions to cover appearance, manner, roles and routines and their related linguistic features.
(2) Use descriptions as part of identification tasks.
(3) Link descriptions to institutional writing in which characteristics are related to specific occupations.

11 DESCRIBING PLACES

When, why and for whom do we write descriptions of places? In personal writing there are such contexts as postcards and letters to friends from abroad, plus descriptions as part of directions on how to go somewhere. In institutional writing, an example such as the following springs to mind:

We have luxury beach hotels with larger, lovelier, lonelier, sunnier beaches than anywhere you can think of. We have buildings and monuments as beautiful as those in any country in Europe, including perhaps the most beautiful building in the world.

Although we may wish to give our students a chance of writing advertising copy like this one on India, and while such writing is amusing, it is of relatively little use to most students and so must be relegated to the ESP classroom.

Another context for describing places is found in guide books and geography textbooks:

A track runs through the centre of Kokorei Village, linking it with Guava in one direction and Piavora in the other. From Piavora, the track rises gently, passing first two houses of the Eagle clan, then on either side of the road two houses belonging to the Iguana clan. Farther along to the right there are two more houses belonging to the Eagle clan, a kitchen and an empty house.

It is this type of description that we will concentrate on in the institutional context, but there is, as we shall see, a considerable overlap with personal writing, particularly with letter writing. For instance, in both institutional and personal writing, a description of place will incorporate a large number of adverbials of location, many in the form of prepositional phrases, such as *on either side of the road. There* sentences also occur with some frequency in such descriptions, e.g. 'There is a large square in the middle of the town.'

As is clear, a description of a place has a strong spatial sense, and such descriptions can be organised according to several principles. The Kokorei text takes a track as the base point for the description, and everything is related to it. This is a commonly used device upon which to write a description, and it can be elaborated by introducing a fictitious visitor who moves along the road or path, the surrounding landscape being viewed through his eyes.

As the visitor enters Kokorei, he climbs the gently rising track, passing first two houses of the Eagle clan, etc.

Spatial boundaries can also form the basis for a description, as can the inter-relationship of things—houses, buildings, settlements

—on the landscape. The type of organising principle depends partly on the purpose of the description. Thus, if the writer is interested in trade connections between settlements, he is likely to take such connections as the basis for his description rather than boundaries or simple, linear relationships.

Whatever the organising principle, it is almost certain that the writer will have a visual representation in mind, and this brings us to the type of visual cue which can be used for such descriptions. A plan or map is the most obvious, though the way we use it depends on the type and topic of the description. If we decide that we want to take a route as the basis for the description of a town or village, then we can use a real or made-up map showing the route of, say, a bus from one part of the town to another. The lesson plan could be as follows:

Lesson 1
(1) Give copies of a map to sub-groups within the Cl.
(2) Distribute copies of a text describing a bus journey. Each sentence will be on a separate slip of paper and the slips will be scrambled.
(3) Tell Cl to put the slips in order according to the route marked on the map.
(4) Refer Cl to BB or OHP version of the map.
 Ask SS to describe the bus journey orally.
(5) Remove copies of the text from Cl.
(6) Give a partially completed version of the text, either on the BB or OHP or on a worksheet.
(7) Tell Cl to write out completed version, using the map as a cue.

Lesson 2
(1) Using the same map, revise the description of the bus journey from A to B, with individual SS contributing.
(2) Tell Cl that they are now going to describe the journey in the *opposite* direction.
 Ask what changes they will have to make. (*Left* becomes *right* and vice versa.)
(3) Have Cl write their own descriptions, using the map as a cue.

(4) Review SS descriptions, focusing particularly on preposition groups and adverbials of location.

Exploitation

Have Cl write similar descriptions using a local bus route or maps as cues. Contextualise by telling them that the description is to be used in a guide book for the use of overseas visitors to your town.

The above lessons have concentrated on the arrangement of items in relation to a route and the description has dealt with places only as they occur on the route concerned. The course of a river could be used for the same type of description. There are, however, other kinds of description which are concerned with an overall view of a landscape as might be obtained from a high peak or an aeroplane. In this case, the organising principle will be somewhat different since the description is concerned with areas within a region rather than with the details of houses and buildings in relation to a given route. Such a description, based on a map like that shown in Figure 8, might take the following form:

From north to south across the region there are five major zones. First there is a narrow coastal plain, immediately behind which there are coastal ranges up to a thousand feet high. Behind these ranges there is a wide zone of intermontane low land, which is intersected by extensive alluvial plains. Finally, there are the inland ranges, running parallel to the coast, and rising to 12,000 feet at the highest point.

Having established the major zones within the region, the writer of this description could then proceed to a detailed description of each zone. In other words, the description moves from a general, overall description to a detailed description of each zone. There is, of course, a logic to such organisation, since it is easier for the reader to make sense of a description which provides the main outlines first before giving the details.

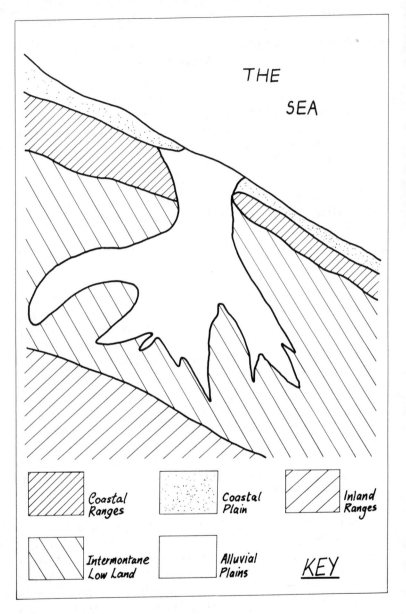

Figure 8

We can present and practise such descriptions using a similar technique to that outlined earlier though with some variation. For instance, instead of breaking the text into component sentences, a map could be provided in which the main zones are shown on separate pieces of paper, or on separate pieces of acetate if you are going to make use of an OHP. The students' task is to arrange these zones according to the description in the text. In other words, it is a kind of jig-saw puzzle. Once the components are correctly arranged, the completed map can be displayed—here the OHP is very useful—and the students can then describe the region from a different viewpoint, e.g. west to east, or north to south.

The jig-saw map idea can be extended for follow-up practice, particularly in conjunction with an OHP, either for small group or individual work. Each group (or student) can be given a packet containing pieces—either on paper or OHP acetate—which show such geographical features as mountains, valleys, plains, and so on. Each group or student can then make up their own landscape with the pieces, assembling them inside a transparent folder so that the pieces remain in place when the completed map is displayed to the rest of the class. Then they can write a description of their landscape, either as a co-operative effort or as individual work. Finally, the landscape maps can be brought to the front of the class and displayed on the OHP. The descriptions can be exchanged around the class, and then students can read the description received, compare it with the maps and match the description with the appropriate map.

The two types of description that we have discussed so far have concentrated on arranging items in a setting, but descriptions may involve more than spatial arrangement, as we see in the following text, modelled on the kind of writing found in guide books:

The visitor now comes to the top of Kendrick Hill where St John's Church is situated. This church, a handsome example of Victorian gothic, dates from 1873. Its spire forms a landmark for miles around. The reredos screen, depicting the Last Supper, is outstanding, while the Lady Chapel contains some fine stained glass. Turning left into St John's Road, the visitor now continues towards the University, passing some fine Victorian mansions to the left . . .

The description not only describes where things are (i.e. location); it also gives information on the things themselves (i.e. objects). While this type of description is particularly common in guide books, it does not require an institutional context to supply examples of such description, as is shown in the following example from personal writing:

Then you come to the top of Kendrick Hill. There's a big church there. You can't miss it. The spire is very tall and you can see it for miles. Well, you turn left at the Church into St John's Road . . .

Descriptive material of this kind can be attached to the spatially organised descriptions which have already been presented and practised. Indeed, the addition of such new items is a useful way of revising earlier material while at the same time adding new content.

Since the description of appearances is now important, maps will have to be supplemented by illustrations or by actual experience. If we use well-known places as the subject of the description, it is an easy matter to obtain photographs, either in the form of postcards or posters. Failing these two sources, illustrations taken from newspapers and magazines may be used. Having obtained the illustrations, you can organise interesting and productive exercises in which the students have to relate the illustration (which will generally be a view from ground level) to the map (which is a plan or overhead view of the same subject). Once the connections between pictures and map have been established, a spatially based description can be devised, with the class contributing suggestions. When this part of the description has been completed, descriptions of individual items in the scene can be elicited from the class, and then these can be slotted into the existing spatially based description. As some of the language features needed for describing things—houses, buildings, monuments, and so on—could already have been practised during lessons on describing objects, there need not be very many unfamiliar items in this lesson. Indeed, the students are now learning to combine already-known items to make something new.

Not all descriptions are concerned with topography and landscape, of course. Geography textbooks are full of descriptions which are about the industries and products of an area. Such descriptions, while still employing the Simple Present tense, often include complex patterns of qualification in the noun phrase, e.g. *the production of sugar cane, the motor industry in the Midlands*. Here is a short text which incorporates these features:

Bristol is an agricultural area. The farm land around Bristol produces 5,000 tons of apples a year. 4,000 tons of those stay in Bristol and 1,000 tons go to other parts of Britain.

This example is linked to information presented in a table of the kind found in geography texts and other sources of information on places and products, such as government handbooks. Part of the table is shown in Table 14.

			tons	stay	go
Bristol	agricultural	apples	5,000	4,000	1,000
Carlisle	agricultural	wool	2,000	1,000	1,000
Port Talbot	industrial	steel	6,000,000	450,000	5,500,000
etc.					

Table 14

Following the model text, and using the information in the table, students can complete other similar paragraphs. It takes little imagination to see the kinds of variation on this theme which can be devised, using information from geography textbooks, atlases, handbooks, newspaper reports, and so on. An even more complex and sophisticated set of writing exercises can be devised using a combination of model text, graphic information (maps, diagrams) and tabulated data (histograms, tables of figures). Fortunately, such information is readily available in the reference section of any library, and since associated maps and diagrams do not usually require great detail, it is possible for even the least artistic teacher to produce simple visual material for use in such exercises.

It is important, however, that there is always a language element to such work. After all, the whole point of the exercise is to improve the students' writing skills and even though graphic information may have to be interpreted verbally, unless the student has the language forms he needs, he will be unable to produce a description which is either correct or appropriate. The provision of a model text helps to give such a guide, and it is perfectly feasible to take some features out of the text—such as the pattern *the + Head Noun + Qualifier*, given above—and to practise a substitution drill using the tabulated information, before going on to incorporate the same pattern in an extended piece of discourse such as that found in the text about Bristol.

Finally, although nearly all the examples we have looked at have concentrated on institutional writing, describing places can provide the basis for personal writing as well. As I suggested at the beginning of this section, postcards and letters to friends are one such context and the exercise reproduced in Figure 9 illustrates how such descriptions can be set in the context of a personal letter. This particular exercise comes at the end of a sequence of exercises in which students have practised the main language items needed for this type of description. They have also used material which has linked a written text to a map so that the transfer of visual and spatial information to verbal form has already been practised. The opening paragraphs of the letter itself have been given in facsimile form so that the teacher can revise lay-out and punctuation conventions as part of the exercise.

DESCRIBING PLACES: SUMMARY

In teaching the writing of description of places:

(1) Focus on location and spatial relationships.
(2) Relate the expression of these relationships to maps and pictures.
(3) Incorporate work on the linguistic expression of location and spatial relationships, notably the adverbial of location.

Describing Places 73

Figure 9   Letters and Map (R. V. White, *Functional English* (Nelson 1979))

On the next page there is a map of Styal village. Styal is in the countryside, several miles from Gatley. When Maria and Carlos came to stay with Tom and Belinda, they visited Styal several times.
Later, Maria wrote a letter to an English friend in Brazil.

(*a*) Read the beginning of Maria's letter.
(*b*) Look at the map of Styal.
(*c*) Use the map of Styal to finish the description in Maria's letter to Jackie. Write two more paragraphs.

> 26 Feltham Road,
> Putney,
> London SW15,
> England.
> 14th May
>
> Dear Jackie,
> Last week we went to Manchester to visit Tom and Belinda. Jason and Alice have grown a lot in the last six months. Jason is taller than our Olavo.
> Tom and Belinda took us to a small village called Styal. It is in the countryside, a few miles from their house. The village has two small churches and some very old cottages.
> You come into Styal village from the main road to Wilmslow, a township two or three miles away. There is a police station on the left and further on there is a village shop. Opposite, on the other side of the road, there is a village butcher's shop, a lovely old pub called the Ship Inn, and a small restaurant.

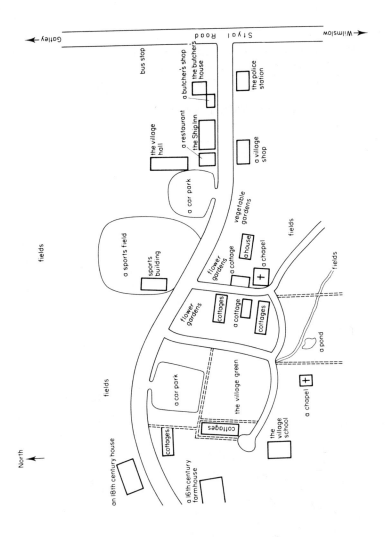

(4) Add other features—such as historical information, architectural and topographical details—as appropriate to your teaching situation.
(5) Contextualise in such institutional contexts as guide books and such personal writing as letters and postcards.

12 DESCRIBING PROCESSES

If we look at how we actually describe *processes*, we find that typically it is associated with the use of the *passive voice*. A process consists of the following elements:

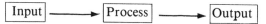

In the process, a raw product is transformed into a finished product. Descriptions of process are very common in scientific and technological writing, although they also occur in everything from advertisements to elementary school textbooks. A receptive and active command of the language used to describe a process is an important part of the repertoire of a very wide range of students. What follows is an account of a series of lessons to practise writing descriptions of processes, using the passive voice.

Lesson 1 (*approximately 40 minutes*)

Aims:
(i) to identify the formal features of the passive voice;
(ii) to relate the use of the passive voice to describing a process;
(iii) to translate a verbal description to diagrammatic form.

Materials:
(i) a text to be read aloud;
(ii) copies of a table to be filled in by SS;
(iii) a BB or OHP copy of a flow diagram to be completed with help from SS.

(1) Tell Cl that they are going to learn how milk is processed. Refer them to the table (see Table 15) that they have been

given. Tell them that they are to listen for all the verbs of the pattern *is produced* while you read the text to them. (Note that some of the verbs are already written in the table as a guide. For reasons of economy, Table 15 includes all of the verbs, though in the actual lesson most of the table would be blank at the beginning.)

Sequencer	Subject	Verb	Adverbial	Full Stop or Comma
	Milk	is produced	on dairy farms	.
	The milk	is delivered	to a factory by tanker	.
	The milk	is weighed		,
and then	it	is tested		.
Next,	the milk	is separated		.
After this	the milk	is pasteurised	at a temperature of 72°F	.
Then	it	is cooled		.
Next	it	is bottled		.
After this,	the bottles	are packed	into crates	.
Finally,	the milk	is delivered	to customers	.

Table 15

(2) Read the text aloud to Cl. Read at a steady pace, pausing between sentences. Do not use contracted forms (e.g. *It's cooled*) at this stage. Read the text a second time to allow SS to check their work, then elicit the verbs from SS and complete the BB or OHP equivalent of their tables.

(3) When the verbs are set out in the table, ask SS to identify the features common to all the verbs. These are, first, that each verb item consists of two elements: *is* or *are* plus past participle, and secondly, that the past participle in this particular text is always the + ed form (i.e. Base + ed).

(4) Following the discussion of the verbal element of the description, continue with a third reading during which SS are to complete the Subject column of their table. Elicit these completions from SS at the end of the reading and complete

Describing Processes 77

the appropriate part of the table.
(5) Give a fourth and final reading, and this time SS complete the remaining parts of their table. Elicit items from Cl and complete table, including the important punctuation column.
(6) When the table is complete, draw attention to the overall organisation of the text, viz. that each sentence describes a step in the process and that the steps are sequentially organised, the sequence being indicated by the sequencers which form the first sentence element. Attention can also be drawn to backward pointing *the*, this being an important cohesive feature of the text. With SS contributing, ring and arrow the text, thus:
Milk is produced . . .
The milk . . .
(7) Refer to the BB or OHP flow diagram. (See Figure 10.) One or two boxes should be completed by way of example, the rest of the diagram being blank.

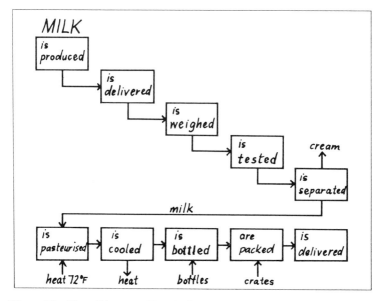

Figure 10   Flow Diagram: How Milk is Processed

(8) Ask SS to give completions for the other boxes.
(9) Discuss the form of the flow diagram, pointing out how it summarises the sequential organisation of the process with each step constituting an input/process/output sequence, the output from one step being the input for the next. Note also how by-products, such as cream, are indicated, while subsidiary inputs, such as heat, bottles and crates, are also shown by appropriate arrows.
(10) Ask SS to read aloud from the completed table of the text. Have each S read more than one sentence since it is important that the interconnection of sentences is stressed and practised.
(11) After two or three turns around the class, obliterate or obscure the completed table and instruct SS to put their own tables away. Then use the completed flow diagram as a cue for oral production.
(12) Instruct SS to reconstitute the text in written form, using the flow diagram as a cue.

You will have noticed that the full passive voice verb group is used in this flow diagram, unlike the one which proved to be a confusing cue for the student whose composition we studied in Section 7 'Good Cues: Bad Results'. The change from flow diagrams incorporating the full passive voice verb group to those labelled with the *Base + ing* form of the verb should be delayed until you are quite sure that the transition will not cause confusion. In fact, in the class of which our unfortunate student was a member, the majority of students could manage to write correct descriptions based on a flow diagram incorporating the *Base + ing* verb as the label for each box, as shown in Figure 1.

Lesson 2

Aims:
(i) to reconstitute a written description of a process from a flow diagram cue;
(ii) to relate changes in the form of the finite verb to changes in number in the Subject of the sentence.

(1) Begin by recapitulating the main points of the previous lesson, viz. the form of the passive verb group, the sequential organisation of a description of process and the use of a flow diagram to summarise such a description.

(2) Refer to the initial element in the passive verb group, taking examples from the milk-processing text. Focus on the following sentences:

The milk is bottled.
The bottles are packed into crates.

(3) Elicit from SS the formal change from *is* to *are* and the change in number of the Subject from singular *milk* to plural *bottles*.

(4) Refer to the flow diagram of fish canning (Figure 11). Ask SS to find a similar change in verb form from *is* to *are*. Then note the change in number of the Subject, from singular *fish* (uncountable) to plural *cans* (countable).

(5) Elicit sentence completions for each step in the process, and complete a BB or OHP table of the description, as shown in Table 16.

Sequencer	Subject	Verb	Adverbial	*Full Stop or Comma*
	Fish	is delivered	to a cannery	.
First,	the fish	is cleaned		,
and then	it	is washed		.
Next	it	is drained		,
and then	it	is soaked	in brine	.
After this	it	is washed	again	,
and then	it	is weighed		.
Next	cans	are filled	with fish	,
and then	liquid	is added	to the cans	.
Then	tops	are attached	to the cans	,
and	the cans	are sterilised		.
After this	the cans	are cooled		,
and then	they	are packed	into cartons	.
Finally,	the cartons	are stored	in a warehouse	.

Table 16

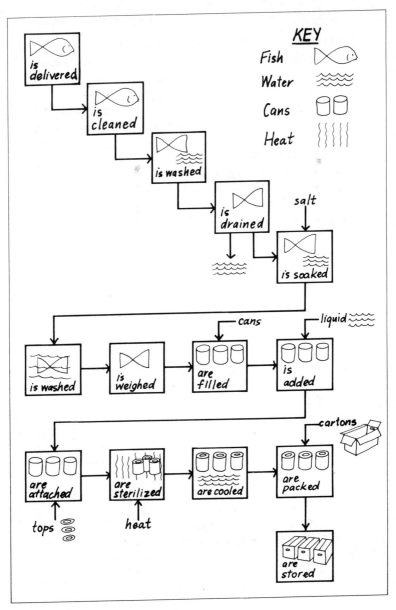

Figure 11 How Fish is Canned

(6) When the table has been completed, elicit reading aloud of the sentences at random round the class. Again, have each S read more than one sentence in sequence so as to practise production of more than one sentence at a time.

(7) Obliterate or obscure the table and ask SS to complete a written description using only the completed flow diagram as a cue. Circulate around the class and check work as it is being done.

It may be useful to draw attention to the punctuation patterns of the sequencers before the students begin to write. Put them up on the BB as follows:

—. Then —.
—, and then —.
—. Next, —.
—. After this, —.
—. Finally, —.

Lesson 3

This lesson can take one of two forms. First, students can be given a description of a process which they have to summarise in flow diagram form. A blank flow diagram with the requisite number of boxes to match the number of steps in the process can be issued as a worksheet. The completed worksheet can then become a cue sheet for written reconstruction of the text. Secondly, a completed flow diagram can be issued to act as a cue sheet for written production. As their teacher, you will be the best judge as to the amount of prompting which the students may need in carrying out either task.

Lesson 4

At this point, two further grammatical items can be studied. These are: (1) the *to* + *Base* verb adverbial of purpose, and (2) the distinction between the active and passive voice. The first of these items can be introduced in context, e.g. The milk is pasteurised at 72°F *to kill* harmful bacteria. Provide students with a text in which several such examples occur. Ask the students to identify them and then point out that such adverbials answer the question 'Why?'. In other words, they state a reason.

The distinction between active and passive can be made by contrasting such statements as:

> Cows *produce* milk on dairy farms.
> and Milk *is produced* on dairy farms.
> Men *weigh* the milk.
> and The milk *is weighed*.

Show how in a process the interest is on the product and the process rather than on the operators and the producers. In any case, in an industrial process the identity of the operatives is usually irrelevant. The passive voice enables us to describe complex industrial processes without having to refer to the people involved in operating the machinery.

Finally, provide the students with a cue sheet from which they have to write a description of a process incorporating several instances of the *to* + *Base* verb adverbial of purpose.

Exploitation

More exercises of the type described above can be used with variation in content and presentation technique. There is no shortage of suitable examples to draw on, since many school textbooks contain descriptions of process, as do such publications as the *Oxford Junior Encyclopaedia* and various titles in the MacDonald Introduction to Technology series. Manufacturing firms also publish descriptions of the processes involved in producing products as diverse as Kellogg's cornflakes and British Steel Corporation steel.

Students can be given a library assignment in which they have to locate a source, abstract a summary, and draw their own flow diagram. Factory visits also provide a splendid exemplification of a process in action, linking language work in the classroom with activity in the real world outside. Preparatory work for a factory visit can involve drawing a table or flow diagram in advance, the students having to fill in the table or diagram with the information they gather during their observation of the process at the factory. Such preparatory work is, in any case, essential since most manufacturing processes involve numerous stages and items of equipment so that unstructured observation—hindered as often as not by the noise of moving machinery—can be very confusing. The impersonality of such industrial processes, a point covered in the contrast between active and passive voice, is well demonstrated by a visit to a factory.

Finally, although I have placed much stress on *industrial* processes, there are processes and procedures in agricultural and pre-industrial cultures which can also be described using the passive voice. The cultivation of rice (in Asia) and the making of tapa cloth (in the South Pacific) are two examples which come to mind. In an English-medium situation, the work of the English and Geography teachers can be complementary in dealing with such topics from their respective viewpoints and can serve to demonstrate to students that the correct and appropriate use of English does not cease at the exit from the English-language classroom.

DESCRIBING PROCESSES: SUMMARY

In teaching the writing of descriptions of processes:
(1) Avoid contrastive presentation of active and passive, as this will confuse students.
(2) Focus initially on the full passive verb phrase.
(3) Make a visual link with the flow diagram, a commonly employed means of summarising processes and procedures.
(4) Draw on and provide institutional contexts found in other subjects in the curriculum and in professional literature.

13 COMPARING AND RECOMMENDING

When and for what purpose do we compare things, people or experiences? One answer to this is when we have to make a choice. There are numerous occasions in daily life when we want 'the bigger one' or 'the cheaper one' or when something 'a little lighter/cooler/cheaper' is required. Little imagination is required to create classroom activities which can be used to teach and practise such comparisons in contexts where the students have to link the appropriate form of the adjective to a choice from an array of alternative objects whose only differentiating characteristic is their size, weight, cost etc. And such practice need not even involve the use of *than*, whose presence can initially cause students to think that comparison is marked by *than* rather than by the form of the adjective.

Yet, even employing such material for oral practice leaves us with the problem of how and what to teach in writing comparisons. When, to begin with, do we *write* comparisons? Again, I think that the answer is when we are concerned with making a choice. Apart from impulse buys, the purchasing of almost anything these days is carried out by many people with due consideration of comparative cost, durability, quality and various other characteristics, and there is an extensive literature in such publications as the Consumers Association's *Which?* magazine to help the would-be purchaser. So, then, we read about comparisons when we are seriously interested in making a purchase—especially if the item concerned is going to cost quite a lot of money—and it follows that the writing of comparisons can take place in the same context, namely, that of comparative surveys of goods and services.

Comparisons do not usually end at saying that B is cheaper than A, however. The reader of consumer surveys is seeking advice as well as information, and although he is usually left to make up his own mind as to the final choice, it is common for the writer to make a conclusion based on the findings of his survey. Thus, writing comparisons logically and authentically leads to another language function within the same context, namely, *making recommendations.*

Let us now turn to seeing how we can go about practising the writing of comparisons and recommendations. We can begin with a text incorporating examples of both functions. This text is modelled on the type of writing we find in survey articles. Some of the more colourful turns of phrase characteristic of some travel writing have been left out so as to highlight the key language items which are being stressed in this section. Likewise, I have substituted letters of the alphabet for real names.

A is a pleasant place for a vacation. During August it has an average temperature of 24°C, and 240 hours of sunshine. Rainfall averages 2 mm. There is a choice of five good hotels, all two star. There are no three star hotels. There is one beach and A has two popular tourist attractions: the ancient town and an old castle.

B is slightly hotter in August, and has more hours of sunshine —225 a month—though average rainfall is lower. It has more good hotels—eight two star and one three star. A has more beaches, but fewer attractions. The market, which is famous for its handicrafts, offers a wide range of local products.

The average summer temperature in C is higher than in A and B, averaging 28°C, while the average sunshine is also higher, though rainfall—1·5 cm—is lower than in A. C has the most places to stay, including two three star hotels, and it has more beaches than A but fewer than B and D. It has some interesting attractions, including some good restaurants, a museum, and lovely villages in the surrounding countryside.

Finally, with an average summer temperature of 30°C, D is the hottest of the four places. It also has the highest average hours of sunshine and the lowest rainfall. D has more hotels than A and B, and there are more first class hotels than at C. D offers the greatest choice of beaches and a range of water sports, including sailing and water skiing.

If you want a place with a good beach and some interesting places to visit, A and C would be a good choice. If you are interested in a more active vacation and like lots of sun and if you don't mind the heat, then D would be a good place to go. However, if you like good food and prefer doing day trips to surrounding places, then C would probably suit you. Finally, if you want to relax on a beach and like to buy souvenirs, B would be a good choice.

A text such as this can provide the basis for a reading comprehension exercise in which the students complete a comparison table with information from the text. Table 17 shows the kind of table which could be issued to students for this purpose.

	A	B	C	D
Average August Temperature, °C		25		
Average Hours of Sunshine		225		
Rainfall, cm		1		
Hotels **		8		
***		1		
Beaches		3		
Other attractions		a market		

Table 17

In the next stage of the lesson, students' attention can be drawn to the ways in which comparisons are made between the four places described in the text. It should be noted that *four* places are given and not three so as to break away from the idea which some students may have that the comparative involves only two items while the superlative is concerned with three. The extent and form of grammatical discussion will obviously depend on the way in which you normally handle grammar and on the expectations of your students. In any event, overt discussion of the formal features involved in comparison should not occupy more than a few minutes because the point of the lesson is not to discuss comparison but to practise it.

In the next practice stage of the lesson, students can write brief paragraphs like the one given below, based on the information in the table which they have completed during the reading comprehension phase of the lesson. When they have made up several such paragraphs, they can swap them with a partner, each member of the pair then having to identify the name of 'X' using the information in the text and the table.

Paragraph
   X has a higher rainfall than B, and fewer beaches than D. It has more hotels than B, but fewer first-class hotels than D. The name of X is —.

Next, shift attention to the form of the recommendations which are made in the final paragraph of the reading text. The key item here is the pattern:

> If you want X, then Y would be + Complement.
>   like   suit
>   prefer

This form of recommendation places the ultimate decision on to the reader, the modal verb (*would*) indicating the tentative nature of the recommendation, while the conditional clause (*if*) indicates the restriction or condition under which the recommendation has been made.

It is possible to organise some formal practice of this item, using substitution drill techniques, but this will not really give the student any insight into the function of such a sentence. For this, more information is needed. If we look at the form of the recommendation, we see that it is related to someone's preferences or *priorities*. Obviously, people's priorities for a vacation vary, and a recommendation must take preferences into account. By listing people and their priorities, we can give students the information they need in order to practise making recommendations, using the information they have already gathered from the first reading text. Table 18 gives a list of such priorities.

Mr X	Mrs Y	Miss K	You
heat	places to visit	choice of beaches	
sunshine	buying souvenirs	choice of good hotels	
sports	good food	lots of sunshine	

Table 18

The priorities can also be presented in the form of a reading passage, with students transferring information to a table; or else they can be given in tabulated form, as in Table 18. Note that space is given in the column for the student himself to list his own priorities. Using these preferences, the student can now match the priorities to the information in the table he completed in the first stage of the lesson. The production of recommendation sentences is now tied to a task in which some discrimination is required on the part of the student. He is doing more than merely manipulate a given sentence pattern, for there is a choice element involved in the recommendation he makes. Furthermore, there is no absolutely wrong or right answer, although logically some choices and recommendations are more appropriate than others. Also, the range of possibilities and the openness of the choices can be varied by limiting or extending the correlation between options available and preferences expressed.

Although in the exercises described above the focus has been on institutional writing, incorporating comparisons and recommendations in personal writing is by no means ruled out. Selecting a suitable place for a vacation, the theme of my example above, can be readily adapted to the context of personal writing, in which the student replies to a request from a 'friend' to advise him or her on the choice of a holiday venue in the writer's own country. The tastes or priorities of the pen friend can be specified and the student then has to describe several suitable places, none of which inevitably will meet all of the correspondent's requirements, before making a recommendation in suitably tentative terms.

Comparing and recommending can also form the basis of a letter to a friend who has asked for advice on such matters as choosing suitable accommodation in the writer's town, buying or selling something (such as a motorcar), undertaking a course of study, deciding on a job, or travelling around the writer's country. The selection of suitable accommodation could be linked to a map in which the characteristics of different areas of the relevant town or city are shown (e.g. proximity to beaches, closeness to industrial areas, access to motorways and metro services, and so on). The student will have to interpret this information in his letter, rather like this:

X is a very attractive suburb. It is nearer to the beach than Y, but is farther from both the motorway and the metro. Also, rents and prices are higher in X, and it is more difficult to find apartments there.

He can then conclude by advising his 'friend' in terms such as these:

If you want to live near the centre of town, and if you don't mind living in an apartment, then I think Z would be a good place to look for somewhere to live. But if you want more space, and don't mind travelling by metro, then B would be better. My family and I have lived here for ten years, and find it very pleasant. Perhaps you would, too!

As you can see, there is a very close link between the language of this example and that of the text at the beginning of this section. The more neutral tone of the earlier institutional example means that we avoid being distracted by the stylistic elements which are appropriate to personal communications, such as the last two sentences in the second paragraph above. It is a comparatively easy matter to add such personal items once the students have mastered the really important skills of comparing and recommending in the context of institutional writing.

As with developing any written communication skill, a great deal of practice is needed, and the problem for the busy teacher is to obtain the information required for such practice. Fortunately, more and more textbooks with a functional or communicative orientation are incorporating displays of information for practice of the kind I have described. But even if you are not yet using such textbooks, there are other published sources from which such information can be drawn. Comparison-based advertisements are quite common nowadays, as we see in Figure 12, while articles in the quality newspapers frequently incorporate graphs, histograms and information displays which are linked to an article whose function is to interpret the information. It is a simple matter either to abstract the information from such sources, or to use the visual display as it is. The fact that the information and its manner of presentation are authentic lends appeal to the material.

In dealing with comparison we have paid particular attention to what one might call 'direct' comparison in which + er and + est adjectives were conspicuous. Comparisons are made in a variety of ways, however, including the following:

Figure 12

TYPE OF CAR	SWAN NATIONAL	AVIS	GODFREY DAVIS
CHEVETTE	WEEKLY UNLIMITED £58.00	WEEKLY UNLIMITED £72.00	WEEKLY UNLIMITED £71.75
CAVALIER (new)	WEEKLY UNLIMITED £72.50	WEEKLY UNLIMITED £90.00	WEEKLY UNLIMITED £89.25
CORTINA ESTATE (new)	WEEKLY UNLIMITED £95.00	WEEKLY UNLIMITED £125.00	WEEKLY UNLIMITED £115.50
CORTINA 1.6 or Automatic 2.0 Ghia	WEEKLY UNLIMITED £95.00	WEEKLY UNLIMITED £140.00	WEEKLY UNLIMITED £115.50
GRANADA 2.8 GL AUTO	WEEKLY UNLIMITED £140.95	WEEKLY UNLIMITED Not available	WEEKLY UNLIMITED £178.50

Taken from current national tariffs. Swan National 12 July 1978. Avis 1st January 1979. Godfrey Davis 9th January 1979.
Rates subject to VAT, and do not include Collision Damage Waiver fee, Personal Accident cover or petrol.
All cars shown above fitted with radio except Godfrey Davis and Swan National Chevette

(1) X is superior to Y.
(2) X is inferior to Y.
(3) The results of B are double those of A.
(4) There has been a 100 per cent increase of C over B.
(5) The Z has doubled.
(6) There has been a decline/fall/drop in D.

Many of these are implied or unstated comparisons, and some, such as (5) and (6), have some past results or figures as a reference point so that even if no actual overt comparison is made, the reader or hearer knows that the fact that A has 'doubled' means 'in comparison with X of a previous time or period'. Implied comparisons of this kind are common in reporting or commenting upon trends or developments, e.g.

In the last five years the number of students taking the English examination has doubled.

In practising such comparisons in writing, it is a good idea to begin by working from a text in which instances are incorporated. A change of strategy may be adopted, however, by asking students to suggest what they might write in order to interpret graphic or tabulated information in which trends or developments over a period are displayed. Here, for instance, in Figure 13 is a graph showing export orders received.

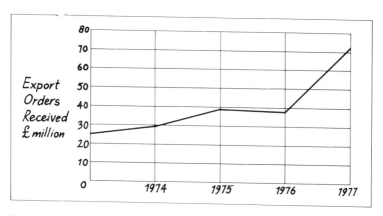

Figure 13

The information in this graph could, of course, be described quite simply like this:

From 1974 to 1975 export orders received rose from nearly 20 million pounds to just under 30 million. There was a slight fall during the period 1975 to 1976, but from 1976 to 1977 the value of orders doubled, and this trend has continued.

You could elicit suggestions from students, drawing on their knowledge of the language acquired in work on reporting and comparing. It would then be possible to introduce some new items, such as:

By 1977 this figure had doubled.
By 1977 there had been a doubling of this figure.

You could provide practice using parallel information so that students could consolidate items already learnt while using new language, such as that suggested in the examples above.

Texts like the ones used here are drawn from institutional writing of the type found in journalism, commercial and business literature and economics and geography textbooks. This link with actual language use in other subjects is, as I have repeatedly stressed, an important consideration in training and practising writing skills. Finding appropriate contexts is no problem if we turn to subjects across the curriculum, and as we have seen, we can remove comparison from the manipulation of trivial content (e.g. 'John is taller than Mary') to the use of real information about the world in which students will actually be using the English writing skills which we have taught them.

COMPARING AND RECOMMENDING: SUMMARY

In teaching the writing of comparisons and recommendations:
(1) Connect comparison with the making of a choice from among similar items.
(2) Link the making of recommendations to a set of priorities or criteria which the recommended item must satisfy.
(3) Use choice and decision situations from the current and future needs of your students.
(4) Find information from published or local sources in which comparison and choice are an important consideration.

14 QUESTIONS AND ANSWERS

In criticising the use of questions as a cueing device, I may have given the impression that questions of any sort are at all times to be banned from the ELT classroom. This is not so. Asking questions (and giving answers) is a skill in its own right, and should not be treated merely as an adjunct to teaching something else. When do we ask questions? Generally when we do not know something which someone else does know. In short, when there is a gap in our information.

The problem for teaching writing is that we write questions much less frequently than we write statements. Thus, it is difficult to find authentic contexts for presenting and practising questions in written form. As I mentioned in Section 10 on 'Describing People', written questionnaires are one context in which written questions occur authentically, and an example is given in Figure 14.

Questionnaires like this one are used in surveys, particularly by manufacturers and service organisations which need to know about the habits, preferences and requirements of the public so that they can produce goods and services that will satisfy public demand.

The Southern Gas questionnaire (Figure 14) was used in a unit on writing questions and answers. It was linked to another text, given below. Students were instructed to read both the text and the questionnaire, and then to answer the items as if they were Mr Adams. Here is the text:

Six months ago Mr Adams bought a large Victorian house in Reading. A month later he asked Southern Gas to give him an estimate for the installation of central heating. He also asked an independent plumber to give him an estimate. After receiving the estimates, Mr Adams decided to ask Mr Duncan, the plumber, to do the installation. Two months ago, Mr Duncan completed the installation of a gas-fired central heating and hot water system. He also connected the gas cooker to the gas supply and made some adjustments to the cooker.

In this exercise the student was given some practice in reading comprehension and in answering questions. In order to provide him with active practice in writing questions, a different procedure must be devised. One obvious technique is to give him the information he wants to obtain and then have him devise questions to elicit the information concerned. Here is an example of this procedure from another exercise:

Set out below are a number of answers to questions about a house to rent. These answers give information on such points as size,

94 Teaching Written English

Marketing Department

P.O. Box 103
Southampton SO9 7GH

Telephone 824124
Telex 477771/2

---

1. Has any type of work been done on your **GAS** appliances in the last three months?

   Yes [ ]   No [ ]

   If **NO**, would you please ignore questions 2 – 4 below and answer question 5 overleaf.

   If **YES**, thinking of the **most recent** job **ONLY** would you kindly complete questions 2 – 5.

---

2. On which appliance was the work done? (Tick appropriate box)

   *Gas central heating [ ]   Gas refrigerator/freezer [ ]

   Gas Cooker [ ]   Gas meter [ ]

   Gas fire or convector [ ]   Other gas appliance (please specify) [ ]

   Gas water heater [ ]

   ....

3. What type of work was done on the appliance?

   *Installed/connected [ ]   Annual Regular Servicing visit [ ]

   Disconnected [ ]   Repair/Maintenance/Service [ ]

   Gas Escape/Emergency [ ]   Any other work (please specify) [ ]

   ....

   *If an appliance was installed/connected was it

   Bought new from Southern Gas [ ]   Bought secondhand [ ]

   Bought new from elsewhere [ ]   Brought from previous home [ ]

                                       Other (please specify) [ ]

   ....

4. Who did you ask to carry out the work?

   Southern Gas [ ]

   Independent company/contractor
   plumber etc. [ ]

   Friend/relative/do-it-yourself [ ]

Figure 14

amenities, and the terms of a lease on the house.

(a) Read this information.
(b) Write questions which will elicit this information.
   Here is an example:

Answer	*Question*
The nearest schools are within half a mile.	*How far is it to the nearest schools?*

(c) Use your questions as the basis for a questionnaire. The questionnaire is to be part of a handbook of advice for overseas visitors who wish to rent a house in Britain. Use a combination of questions and boxes for ticking as in the Southern Gas questionnaire.
   Here is an example:

   What amenities does the house have?

   Washing machine ☐
   Refrigerator ☐
   Deep freeze ☐
   Central heating ☐
   Other (specify)..........................

(1) 289 Sunbury Avenue, Slough.
(2) £140.00 per month.
(3) The nearest schools are within half a mile.
(4) The shops are at the top of the street.
(5) There is a bus route to the centre of town at the bottom of the street.
(6) There is a park and children's playground 5 minutes' walk away.
(7) There is a large sitting room, a small dining room, a kitchen, three bedrooms, a separate bathroom and w.c. There is also a small utility room behind the garage.
(8) There is an automatic washing machine, a tumble drier, and a refrigerator. The house has gas-fired central heating and double-glazing throughout. There is a telephone and television.
(9) There is a small garden—10 metres by 15 metres.
(10) The tenant is responsible for maintaining the garden. There are garden tools for this purpose.

(11) The tenant is responsible for paying telephone bills.
(12) The tenant is responsible for paying the television licence.
(13) The tenant is responsible for paying local property rates.
(14) Sub-letting to another tenant is not permitted.
(15) Two references are required. One of these should be from a bank.
(16) A deposit equivalent to one month's rent is payable in advance. This deposit is returnable on satisfactory completion of the lease.
(17) Rent is payable in advance on the last day of each month.
(18) The lease is for a period of 18 months.
(19) The tenant has to supply bed linen and towels.

In the examples just given, the student has had to practise a range of question types, predominantly inversion questions with a question word, e.g. Who did you ask to carry out the work? These are relatively advanced questions, and it is probably best first to establish inversion questions *without* a question word, e.g. Do you live in London? Also, students will be less confused if they deal with one question type at a time. Even within such a linguistically simple format, it is possible to produce a questionnaire which is both sophisticated and authentic in content and style. An example of such a questionnaire taken from the end of a unit in which much of the practice has been on spoken questions is given in Figure 15.

After using the questionnaire themselves, students then go on to devise their own questionnaire on a topic of current or local interest. This can, incidentally, involve useful practice of expressions of opinion and making suggestions during the discussion on the choice of topic and the types of questions which should be incorporated in the questionnaire. Once agreement has been reached on the information being sought and on a general outline of the questionnaire, individual students or small groups can complete their own questionnaire and then compare and use the final versions.

A questionnaire should not remain unused, partly because students will feel rather cheated if they have produced something which is not exploited, but mostly because the answers to the

Thames College of Further Education Language Questionnaire

Introduction
The college is carrying out a survey among foreign language students in order to help with course planning for next year. We would be grateful for your help. Please answer the questions set out below.

1 Are you aged between   16 and 18 ☐   18 and 20 ☐   20 and 25 ☐
                          25 and 30 ☐   30 and 40 ☐   40 and 50 ☐

2 Do you have a full-time or part-time job, or are you a full-time student?
   Full-time ☐ In full-time ☐ Part-time ☐ Not   ☐ Other   ☐
   employed   education   employed   employed   (Tick and
                                                          state)
   _____

3 Do you earn between   £1 and £2,000 per year? ☐   £2 and £3,000 per year? ☐
                         £3 and £4,000 per year? ☐   £4 and £5,000 per year? ☐
                         £5 and £10,000 per year? ☐

4 Does your employer pay your fees?   Yes ☐   No ☐

5 Does your employer give you time off to come to classes?   Yes ☐   No ☐

6 Is your firm in retailing and wholesaling ☐   manufacturing ☐   banking ☐   travel ☐   Other ☐
                                                                                          (Tick and state)
   _____

7 Does your company trade with foreign countries?   Yes ☐   No ☐

8 Does your company send you overseas on business?   Yes ☐   No ☐

9 Does your company pay higher salaries to employees who speak a foreign language?   Yes ☐   No ☐

10 Do you know any other foreign language?   Yes ☐   No ☐

Figure 15   Questionnaire for Thames College of Further Education
(R. V. White, *Functional English* (Nelson 1979))

questions can be analysed and the findings used as the basis of a written exercise. For instance, answers to the language questionnaire given above could be used to write a description of the class. Information needed for a description of a person, occupation or activity can also be elicited by questionnaire, as suggested in an earlier section, and subsequently used to write a report.

So, then, questions and answers do have a valid place in the writing programme. Even very closely controlled spoken and written practice, not unlike a pattern drill in format, can be linked to the communicative use of questions to elicit required information. In this way, questions and answers achieve a status of their own and some of the problems which arise from using questions as a cueing device are avoided.

QUESTIONS AND ANSWERS: SUMMARY

In teaching the use of questions and answers for both personal and institutional writing:

(1) Make sure that questions are used for a real communicative purpose, viz. to elicit information which the questioner does not know.
(2) Have students practise the authentic form of answer to the questions that they are asked—this often means *not* answering in a full sentence.
(3) Provide information in an organised form as a basis for appropriate question and answer practice.
(4) Use the questionnaire as an authentic context for practising the formation and use of questions and responses in the written medium.

15 DICTATION AND WRITING

Dictation has had a somewhat chequered history during the last decade or so. Traditionally, a dictation required the student to write down every word of what the reader said, and a dictation test was often a much feared part of public examinations. Then, for some time dictation fell into disfavour, and there certainly are very good reasons for questioning the value of word-by-word transcription. With the exception of stenographers, this is a skill which very few of us ever have to practise outside of the language classroom. What we do have to carry out, though, is note-taking in which it is necessary to identify key pieces of information and to record them in an economical and coherent form. Consequently, word-by-word dictation has tended to be replaced by note-taking linked to the development of listening comprehension skills.

In making this shift towards more utilitarian skills, we should not lose sight of the value of carefully structured and restricted 'listen and write' exercises which are variants on dictation. As I have stressed in the preceding sections, in order to write it is necessary to have something to write about. The information upon which the student can base his writing may be presented in a variety of ways, of which the spoken medium is one. Furthermore, listening for particular language items can be a way of sharpening the students' perception of formal language features, a control of which—both receptive and productive—will be necessary for a functional command of the language.

Although I have stressed the importance of promoting practice in writing discourse (as opposed to individual, unrelated sentences), there is one area which causes foreign students a great deal of difficulty, and that is in translating spoken figures into written form. This is hardly surprising, because even the most 'balanced' of bilinguals will always prefer to count in one language rather than another, and foreign figures, like foreign currency, tend to be meaningful only when translated into our native language equivalent. So, then, a simple but effective form of dictation involves numbers. This can be done by reading aloud numbers which the students have to write down in number form, thus: 'three hundred and forty-nine' (spoken) becomes 349 (written).

As a time filler at the end of a lesson, this kind of number dictation has its uses. A more appealing and more challenging form, however, involves arithmetical problems. The teacher reads aloud an arithmetical problem, such as 'three hundred and forty-nine minus fifty-seven', and the students have to write this down in numerical form (349—57) and produce the answer, also in numerical form. This exercise type can be made more challenging if the arithmetical exercise is embedded in a story, such as the following:

> *Mme Loiselle's flight was due to arrive at Heathrow at 9.35 in the morning. Unfortunately, there was a fog. As a result, her flight was cancelled and she travelled via Prestwick. She finally touched down at Heathrow four and a half hours later than her original arrival time. What time did she arrive there?*

The report of this sequence of events is read to the class, and students have to note the original time of arrival, the period of the delay, and on the basis of these two pieces of information, they then have to work out the actual arrival time. Variations on this theme, using measurements of time, quantity, space and weight, have been found to be very effective, and as is obvious from the example just given, they can be related to the teaching of such functions as reporting the past, comparing, describing, and so on.

Focused dictation—that is, dictation which focuses on one language item at a time—can be used to practise formal features of the language, such as verb and noun forms, sentence patterns and collocations. The section dealing with describing processes provided examples of focused dictation in which students had to attend to the teacher's reading aloud of a text in order to identify key items in a related sequence. The same technique can be used to give practice in the correct construction of complex verb groups. For instance, you read aloud the following text while students are instructed to write down the verbs which follow *must* or *should*.

Text
> *When going abroad, you must carry a passport. You must obtain visas for entry permits if these are required. You must also have vaccinations and you should check requirements before you travel. Finally, you should carry your money in travellers' cheques.*

The students would be provided with a sequenced list, as shown below, to which they add the appropriate lexical verbs as they hear them.

(1) must —
(2) must —
(3) must —
(4) should —
(5) should —

Listening and writing need not be the end of the exercise, of course, because the verb groups (as they now are once the student has added the main verb) can be used as the basis for reconstituting the original text. This could be done by asking students to tell you which things are obligatory *must* and which things are recommended *should*, thus:

Obligatory	*Recommended*
carry a passport	check vaccination requirements
obtain entry permits	carry your money in travellers' cheques
have vaccinations	

It will not escape the notice of the alert student that the entries in the above lists take the form of *instructions*, in which the *Base* form of the verb is used. This, in fact, is one of the points of the exercise: to give students practice in using the bare infinitive in association with modal verbs like *must* and *should*, since errors like 'must to obtain' are not unheard of in the written and spoken production of even quite advanced students.

Other dictation exercises can be given on simple verb forms, particularly the Past tense. Once some practice has been given on applying such spelling rules as 'verbs ending in *y* change to *ied* in the Past tense', students can be supplied with a short list of verbs in the infinitive form which they have to write in the form in which they hear them in the dictation passage. Obviously, to give some point to the exercise, not all of the verbs in the list will be in the Past tense or *Base* + *ed* form, otherwise students could simply write them all out in the correct past form without having to listen to the passage. The completed verb list can then be used as a cue to reconstruct the story.

The verb phrase is not the only language item which can be the focus for such activity, of course. The *noun phrase* in English is very complicated for the foreign learner because there is an almost infinite combination of items which can come both before *and* after the Head Noun. Dictation work can be used to focus attention on the ordering of elements by giving students a number of noun groups in which the items for each group are in scrambled form. Here is a complete noun group—*the function of the handle*—in scrambled form: *handle   the   of   function*. As students listen to the text, they number the elements of each group in the order in which they hear them, thus: 5 *handle*   1 *the*   3 *of*   2 *function*   4 *the*. The completed noun groups are then written out with the elements in the correct sequence, thus: *the function of the handle* etc. Once the noun groups have been written out correctly, the passage can be read again, and students can listen for other information needed to produce a complete version of the text. In the above example, the complete sentence would read 'The function of the handle is to provide leverage'.

There are, in fact, certain *collocations* in the noun phrase which are common and which provide the learner with some difficulty. Focused practice in the use of various collocations can be provided by using variations on the techniques of selective listening that I have already described. In addition to giving practice in listening for and writing down words which come *before* a given item (such as + *ed* adjectives or classifiers in such noun groups as *the boiled water*), practice can be provided in listening for words which come *after* nominated items. Quite often these words are prepositions, and since these are almost always unstressed (and therefore difficult to perceive), dictation which focuses students' attention on them has an obvious value.

Finally, a passage can be given in cloze form in which every nth word (usually every 7th word) has been omitted and a gap or space left. Before (or after) the students attempt to fill the gaps in the text, the passage can be read aloud to them. They should not follow the written version of the text as it is read, however, since this would make the exercise excessively simple. Instead, if the text is read aloud to them before they read it themselves, they can rely on memory to help them to reconstruct the mutilated written text that they have been given. They can, of course, read the cloze passage before they listen to the reading. Alternatively, they can attempt to complete the cloze text and then they can listen to it being read aloud as a means of checking their own completion.

As I hope to have shown, dictation can be a useful means of giving written practice linked to oral input. By definition, dictation is *controlled*, because the student is required to write down the *exact* words from the spoken text. The important difference between the kinds of dictation exercise I have outlined above and the type which used to be traditional is that in the ones just described, the student is required to attend only to *one* kind of item at a time. In other words, his *listening* is *selective*. To overcome the objection that his listening may be so selective that he fails to attend to the meaning of the text, it is a good idea always to read the text more than once for *meaning* as well as form. Also, the exploitation work which follows the dictation exercise can be such as to demand more than a fragmentary hearing of the original passage.

In reading a text, care should be taken not to adopt an artificially controlled form of delivery. Although the delivery should not be too fast, it should allow natural stress and intonation. In other words, function words such as prepositions and articles should be unstressed (as they naturally are), and morphological features, such as verb inflections, should not be exaggerated. The pace of the actual dictation reading (when students are supposed to be writing or noting items) may be slower than the review reading (when students can check what they have done in the previous hearing). Throughout, the emphasis is to be on as natural a use of the language as possible, and the dictation exercises described provide a good opportunity for making use of native English-speaking colleagues or visitors, who can record a stock of short dictation texts for subsequent use. Since such texts can—and, indeed, usually are—based on written rather than spoken English, the provision of texts presents far fewer problems than we encounter when attempting to assemble a stock of authentic spoken texts for listening comprehension exercises.

DICTATION AND WRITING: SUMMARY

For controlled practice linking speech and writing, dictation can be used to

(1) Focus students' attention and perception on formal features of the language.
(2) Train selective listening.
(3) Develop note-taking skills.
(4) Provide information or language for further written practice.

16 INTEGRATING READING, SPEAKING, LISTENING AND WRITING

As will have become clear from the examples discussed in the previous sections, I am very much in favour of integrating the so-called four skills in such a way that what is read or what is listened to supplies both a model and information for what is to be written by the student. Clearly, there are limitations to the extent to which such integration is possible. For instance, it is pointless asking students to write dialogues because this does not represent an authentic writing task—unless one is teaching script writers or playwrights. Also, for reasons I have suggested in the introduction to this book, teaching creative writing in the EFL/ESL classroom is of questionable value, and should not be confused with teaching the communicative writing skills which the majority of our students require.

The integration of skills can follow the procedure summarised in Figure 16. First, the students are presented with a spoken or written text which provides a model of linguistic form as well as communicative function. The students' task is to abstract nominated items from the text. These will normally be pieces of *information* (the comprehension element) as well as items of

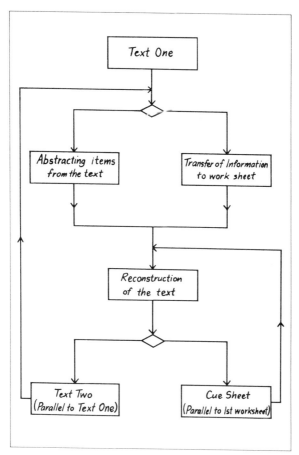

Figure 16 Integrating the Four Skills

language (the formal or structural element). The provision of a worksheet for this exercise focuses and organises the students' task. The worksheet may involve transferring information from the verbal form of the original to a visual counterpart, and examples of this have been given in earlier sections, notably with reference to narrative and describing processes.

The summary of the original communication now becomes the cue or prompt for reconstruction of the text. Such reconstruction may differ from the original text, particularly if the original has been in spoken form. The nature of the reconstruction will be determined by the form of the worksheet/cue sheet and the scope of the task which you have set the class. This task should not, of course, follow the crippling prescription of the traditional précis, viz. 'rewrite this passage in X words'.

These first two stages are now followed by a choice of procedures. Either you can give the students a second text, paralleling the first, or else you can provide a visual or a cue sheet which parallels the one they have already completed on the basis of the first text. This second cue sheet will supply the information needed by the student to produce a communication of his own along the lines of the original text. The purpose of the original text is, of course, to provide a model, but this does not mean that the student should simply slavishly imitate the original. The opportunity for individual variation may be determined by the degree of 'openness' or 'closeness' of the cue which you give the student, and in any case, the sequence of writing exercises will move from control to freedom during the course of lessons devoted to a given language function and type of writing.

The emphasis on continuous pieces of writing should not obscure the need to provide practice on individual structural or functional items. Indeed, the focus of a lesson may well be on one or two formal features within a given functional context (e.g. Past tense verb forms and preposition phrases as part of narrative). But even if students are given writing tasks which are intended to reinforce a given structural or functional item, they should always have subsequent practice of using the item concerned in a longer stretch of discourse. This stricture applies at all levels, and is well demonstrated at a relatively advanced level by Keith Johnson's *Communicate in Writing* in which recognition and reinforcement practice of individual items leads to the writing of extended pieces of prose in which these items are embodied.

17 CORRECTING WRITTEN WORK

Although there is much emphasis nowadays on the concept of

teacher as facilitator, there is one important function which normally only the teacher can perform, and that is his role in monitoring standards of *accuracy* and *appropriateness*. What this means in practical terms is that we teachers are the ones who mark the students' work. Or are we? The answer is, not necessarily so. The students themselves can check each other's work, though this does not mean that we can take a holiday from marking.

The first point to make about marking is that the writing lesson should always be organised in such a way that the students' attention is focused on key items so that they know what it is that they should be getting right. There are, after all, so many things to keep in mind when writing that it is difficult completely to control everything at once, particularly if new items are being practised. We do not need a psychologist to tell us that our attention cannot simultaneously focus on several things and it makes sense to direct the students to check their work for a given, limited number of items.

Normally students should check each sentence to make sure that it contains a *finite verb*. (We do not need to use this term, of course. We can use an expression such as 'a word like *travelled*' or 'a group of words like *is weighed*'.) Then, depending on the language function or functions which are the point of the exercise, students can be instructed to check for other formal items, such as the presence (or absence) of articles before singular countable (or uncountable) nouns, the correct use of backward pointing *the*, the use of prepositions in adverbials of location, and so on.

This checking procedure can be simplified during the early stages of teaching writing by having students write a first draft in a table, like those shown in Tables 9 and 10. Once students have checked their sentences in such tables, they can write out their fair copies as a continuous paragraph or paragraphs. Such a procedure may appear to be excessively mechanistic, but experience of using it with 'false beginners' suggests that rigorously applied over the course of a year, one effect is to train students to write simple, accurate sentences which avoid the tendency of such learners towards the complicated and incomprehensible. Furthermore, since each space in the table should usually have something in it, one can give particular attention to the well-known tendency of some students (e.g. Spanish speakers) to omit the Subject of the sentence, or of others (e.g. Arab learners) to show great disregard for the conventions of punctuation.

It is also wise to check student work as it is being done by circulating around the classroom and looking over students' shoulders as they write. This procedure has two advantages: it can lighten your load of take-home marking, and it enables you to identify any common or general areas of difficulty so that you can take remedial action with the whole of the group there and then. I usually make it a habit to tick each student's piece of writing at the point he has reached when I have looked at it. This means that when I look at his work again, I do not have to go back over the section I have already read and marked.

In marking work, it is now generally agreed that one should avoid covering the page with a sea of red ink. It is a good idea to develop a marking code, with such symbols as *T* for tense, *V* for verb form, *P* for preposition, and so on. There are limitations to such a code, of course. For one thing, it implies that your students know what a verb is, and for another, it is not always possible to distinguish between what might be called a 'tense' error and what could equally well be called a 'verb form' error, and so on. Even so, some sort of code is preferable for all concerned, so long as both teacher and student are in agreement on what the code means.

The use of a code does not absolve us from marking with discretion, however. It is quite likely that students will make a number of different types of error, but it will be fruitless to concentrate on all of them, either when marking or in a remedial or correction lesson. It is best to let the students know what you are going to mark for. Normally this will be the main language point or points associated with the writing that they are practising. This does not mean that you should ignore any other errors which occur. Rather, it is a matter of priorities and of avoiding that well-known phenomenon of running in several different directions simultaneously, to everyone's confusion.

Once students' work has been checked, they should correct the errors which they have made. If the error is common to many students, some remedial practice may be given in the next language class. If the error is confined to a small number of individuals, it may be useful to give them a remedial exercise for homework, rather than bore the rest of the class by going over something which they have got correct. These fortunate students can, of course, assist in the monitoring and correcting process, and pair or group correction is one way of putting the responsibility for checking on to the students themselves.

Finally, if as may be the case, your students have consistently made an error, some general remedial work is called for. The main and perhaps only point to make here is that the remedial work should absolutely *not* be more of the same work as they have already done. Quite clearly, it did not work the first time, and it is even less likely to work second time round. If you have inherited a remedial problem, your task is made easier to the extent that you probably will give your students work which is different from that which they did with their previous teachers. If, however, you are dealing with your own remedial problem, that is, one resulting from your own teaching, then you will need to rethink your approach to the item concerned. This may mean planning some new lessons or finding new published material. And do not be discouraged or discouraging. We can learn a lot from our students' errors, for they are often a better guide to how to improve our teaching than our successes, which frequently pass unnoticed.

18 SUMMARY

In teaching writing in both personal and institutional contexts:

(1) Integrate writing with other activities: speaking, listening, reading.
(2) Use information and/or language acquired through one source (e.g. silent reading) as the basis for writing practice.
(3) Specify the main aims of a writing exercise so that the students know what it is that they should give most attention to.
(4) Mark for and correct these main items.

(5) Encourage students in self-checking and self-correcting.
(6) Do not confuse and discourage students by intensive and unselective marking of items not related to the main aims of the writing task you have set.
(7) Adopt quite different procedures in remedial work from those which have been used in previous teaching.

References

You may want to read some more about writing at a more academic level. If so, I would recommend:

A. Davies and H. G. Widdowson, 'Reading and writing', in *The Edinburgh Course in Applied Linguistics*, Vol. 3, edited by J. P. B. Allen and S. Pit Corder (London, Oxford University Press, 1974).
H. G. Widdowson, *Teaching Language as Communication* (London, Oxford University Press, 1978).

In his book, Widdowson draws on examples from ESP, notably the *English in Focus* series, of which he is an editor. In common with many other ESP materials, the Focus series contains some interesting ideas for training reading comprehension and practising writing, and you may find it helpful to look at titles in this series as well as at other ESP course materials.

English in Focus (London, Oxford University Press).
Nucleus, edited by Martin Bates and Tony Dudley-Evans (London, Longman).
John Swales, *Writing Scientific English* (Sunbury-on-Thames, Nelson, 1971).

It is unfortunate for the teacher of beginners that much of the best work on the teaching of writing has either been in the context of ESP or of teaching advanced learners. Textbooks which emphasise the organisation of writing on a conceptual or functional basis are as follows:

Janelle Cooper, *Think and Link* (London, E. Arnold, 1979).

John Arnold and Jeremy Harper, *Advanced Writing Skills* (London, Longman, 1978).

Maurice Imhoof and Herman Hudson, *From Paragraph to Essay* (London, Longman, 1975).

Keith Johnson, *Communicate in Writing* (London, Longman, 1980).

Mary S. Lawrence, *Writing as a Thinking Process* (Ann Arbor, Michigan, University of Michigan Press, 1972).

At elementary and pre-intermediate level, there are very few up-to-date textbooks on writing, and those titles which are available tend to reflect earlier approaches to the teaching of this skill. Even so, such publications can be adapted to more communicative use, and the illustrations can form the basis of newly devised writing exercises along the lines I have suggested. Such titles as the following are representative:

Donn Byrne, *Progressive Picture Compositions* (London, Longman, 1967).

J. B. Heaton, *Composition through Pictures* (London, Longman, 1966).

L. A. Hill has also produced a number of guided picture composition books for Oxford University Press, though some of these are very dated now. An up-to-date book by him is:

L. A. Hill, *Writing for a Purpose* (London, Oxford University Press, 1978).

At intermediate plus level there is:

D. H. Spencer, *Guided Composition Exercises* (London, Longman, 1967).

Although published over ten years ago, this is still very good value and can be used as an effective supplement to any course book which devotes most time and emphasis to the practice of the spoken language. Also very useful are:

T. C. Jupp and John Milne, *Guided Paragraph Writing*, and *Guided Course in English Composition* (London, Heinemann, 1972 and 1969).

If you want writing exercises as an integral part of a general course, you will find the following worth looking at:

Brian Abbs and Ingrid Freebairn, *Strategies* (London, Longman, 1977).

Donn Byrne and Susan Holden, *Insight* and *Outlook* (London, Longman, 1978)

Ronald V. White, *Functional English*: Book 1, *Consolidation*, Book 2, *Exploitation* (Sunbury-on-Thames, Nelson, 1979).

Some of the examples I have referred to in this book have been taken from *Functional English* and there are also some parallels with exercises in *Strategies*.

An imaginative approach to teaching varieties of writing is provided by:

Donn Byrne and Susan Holden, *Follow Through* (London, Longman, 1978).

Two very useful sources of ideas and information for writing exercises are:

H. M. Dobson, *Basic Skills You Need* (Sunbury-on-Thames, Nelson, 1976).

B. J. Thomas, *Practical Information* (London, Edward Arnold, 1977).

If you want to obtain some more ideas on using dictation, you will find some useful suggestions in the following article, which I drew on in Section 15 on 'Dictation and Writing':

Dorothy Brown and Helen Barnard, 'Dictation as a learning experience', *RELC Journal* (Singapore), Vol. 6, No. 2, pp. 42-62.

A useful discussion on correcting written work, with particular emphasis on group correction, can be found in the following article:

C. Brumfit, 'Correcting written work', *Modern English Teacher*, Vol. 5, No. 3, pp. 22-3.

Finally, if your particular problem is the teaching of handwriting (or script), you are not very well provided for, though you can refer to the following:

J. A. Bright and R. Piggott, *Handwriting, A Workbook* (London, Cambridge University Press, 1976). There is an accompanying teacher's book by J. A. Bright.

B. H. Seward, 'Teaching cursive writing to EFL students', *English Language Teaching*, Vol. 26, No. 2, pp. 169-78.